NEW DIRECTIONS FOR PROGRAM EVALUATION
A Publication of the American Evaluation Association

Nick L. Smith, *Syracuse University*
EDITOR-IN-CHIEF

Multisite Evaluations

Robin S. Turpin
Lutheran General Health Care System

James M. Sinacore
Northwestern University Medical School

EDITORS

Number 50, Summer 1991

JOSSEY-BASS INC., PUBLISHERS, San Francisco

MAXWELL MACMILLAN INTERNATIONAL PUBLISHING GROUP
New York • Oxford • Singapore • Sydney • Toronto

MULTISITE EVALUATIONS
Robin S. Turpin, James M. Sinacore (eds.)
New Directions for Program Evaluation, no. 50
Nick L. Smith, Editor-in-Chief

© 1991 by Jossey-Bass Inc., Publishers. All rights reserved.

Microfilm copies of issues and articles are available in 16mm and 35mm, as well as microfiche in 105mm, through University Microfilms Inc., 300 North Zeeb Road, Ann Arbor, Michigan 48106.

LC 85-644749   ISSN 0164-7989   ISBN 1-55542-796-0

NEW DIRECTIONS FOR PROGRAM EVALUATION is part of The Jossey-Bass Education Series and is published quarterly by Jossey-Bass Inc., Publishers (publication number USPS 449-050).

EDITORIAL CORRESPONDENCE should be sent to the Editor-in-Chief, Nick L. Smith, School of Education, Syracuse University, 330 Huntington Hall, Syracuse, New York 13244-2340.

Printed on acid-free paper in the United States of America.

619647

American Evaluation Association, 9555 Persimmon Tree Road, Potomac, MD 20854

CONTENTS

EDITORS' NOTES

Several years ago we both were part of a research team that was approached by members of the U.S. Congress to develop a series of large-scale process evaluations. In particular, the House Subcommittee on Veterans Affairs wanted to know if, as alleged by many rumors, eligible veterans were being denied health care by the Veterans Administration (now called the Department of Veterans Affairs). Needless to say, the planning of evaluations at 172 medical centers and 36 outpatient clinics in all fifty states and Puerto Rico was a tremendous challenge, and we clearly could have used guidance on how to accomplish this task. Try as we might, however, we were unable to locate any literature that addressed the problems intrinsic to evaluating programs implemented at different geographical locations. Since then, we have worked together and independently on other, similar evaluations and have encountered a number of colleagues who are engaged in the same task. Because evaluations of programs at multiple sites seem to be relatively common, we have come to classify them as *multisite evaluations* (MSEs).

It appears that many evaluators conduct MSEs for similar reasons: to increase generalizability of findings, to maximize sample size, and to respond to a variety of political and social demands. In conducting these evaluations, we all must struggle with the same organizational, procedural, and statistical issues, yet we have little (if any) opportunity to learn from the insight of others or to share our own experiences. Although we have found that there is a growing body of literature in the area of multisite clinical trials, this information is not written for evaluators, nor is it directly applicable to evaluation research, which has its own methodological concerns and sensitivities.

This volume, *Multisite Evaluations,* was born out of the need to provide a guide to evaluators who are planning or conducting MSEs. Although it does not address all of the issues, viewpoints, problems, and topical areas, we hope that it will open a dialogue with other evaluators and encourage more work in the area. We have just begun to develop and adapt evaluation techniques for use with multiple sites and there is still much work left to be done. But we are confident that this type of evaluation is becoming quite common. In fact, the Department of Veterans Affairs has recently funded two permanent centers devoted to multisite studies in health services research.

Overview of the Chapters

When we began to solicit contributions for this volume, we contacted colleagues who we knew were conducting MSEs or who were familiar with published multisite work in their areas of expertise. Our aim was to construct a volume that discussed MSEs in relation to different disciplines. We therefore sought contributions in health care, criminal justice, education, public policy, mental health, and industry.

As we read chapter proposals, we discovered that the central methodological and organizational problems of MSEs are primarily universal. In other words, we found that evaluators confront similar issues irrespective of their academic disciplines. We therefore gave primary attention to these universal issues, as opposed to discipline-specific issues, when we arranged the chapters in the volume.

All of the chapters in this volume are organized in a similar way. Each begins with a synopsis of the issues or topics discussed, followed by details and examples. Our opening chapter proposes a definition of MSEs and presents an overview of the benefits and challenges that are characteristic of this form of evaluation. We provide an overview of organizational concerns, such as staffing and quality control, and of methodological issues, such as generalizability and statistical analysis.

In Chapter Two, Susan C. Hedrick and her colleagues refer to their experience with an adult day health care program to describe how a successful MSE depends on a balance of centralized and decentralized staffing and direction. They note that some aspects of the evaluation, such as quality control, should be managed by a central office coordinator; while other aspects, such as recruitment, can be handled by a site coordinator.

In Chapter Three, Albert J. Reiss, Jr., and Robert Boruch provide additional ideas about the management of a multisite study by describing the Program Review Team approach. This approach is unique in that the members of the team guide the ongoing success of a MSE in an interactive fashion. They do not simply act as an advisory board but rather periodically review the progress of each site, conduct preliminary analyses of data, and examine findings across sites. The authors note that this type of approach provides quality information to program sponsors and promotes sound policy advice and good science.

In Chapter Four, Carol T. Mowbray and Sandra E. Herman describe how the implementation of programs at multiple sites adapts to local needs and circumstances. They note, however, that extensive adaptation can compromise the implementation model. If this occurs, one will no longer have an evaluation of a single program at multiple sites but instead a series of evaluations of different interventions.

In Chapter Five, Phoebe H. Cottingham extends the main idea of the preceding chapter by discussing the importance of analyzing program effects on a site-by-site basis, especially when there are implementation differences across the sites. Based on an evaluation of job-training programs for single mothers, the author discovered that strong site-specific differences would have been missed if the data from all locations had been lumped together for a single analysis.

Chapters Six, Seven, and Eight conclude the volume by addressing qualities of systems that impede and promote MSEs. These three chapters deal with different domains, yet each leads us to think about the attributes within our own areas or disciplines that can affect evaluation in negative or positive ways.

In Chapter Six, Stephen J. Guastello and Denise D. Guastello discuss the dimensions of organizational structure and climate. Their main point is that organizations have "personalities" that can affect the outcomes of evaluations. Therefore, one needs to consider these dimensions before conducting a MSE.

In Chapter Seven, Wesley G. Skogan and Arthur J. Lurigio describe the social, political, and organizational characteristics of the criminal justice system that make MSEs difficult. They note, for example, that policing agencies foster a subculture of secrecy that shields them from public view. This subculture fosters an "us-against-them" mentality toward evaluators who are viewed as snoops for management, the courts, or political opportunists.

Finally, in Chapter Eight, Jay A. Freedman discusses the technical, historical, and political features of the health care system that promote MSEs—for example, the availability of large, multisite, health care data bases, the growth of multi-institutional health care systems, and the history of multisite biomedical clinical trials. This chapter ends the volume on a positive note. Namely, MSEs constitute an evaluation research methodology that is keeping pace with the ways in which human services programs are implemented. As such, MSEs clearly represent a new direction for program evaluation.

Conclusion

The conduct of MSEs requires careful consideration. There are advantages and limitations on organizational, methodological, and personal levels. MSEs are becoming popular, and an increasing number of evaluators will soon have to demonstrate the skills necessary to conduct such evaluations. This volume is presented as a source to which people can turn to prepare themselves for this most challenging form of evaluation research.

Robin S. Turpin
James M. Sinacore
Editors

Robin S. Turpin is senior coordinator, Research and Sponsored Programs, for Lutheran General Health Care System in Park Ridge, Illinois. She was formerly senior health scientist at the Health Services Research and Development Field Program of Hines Veterans Administration Hospital. She is a social psychologist and is adjunct faculty in the Department of Psychology at Loyola University Chicago.

James M. Sinacore is statistician and research associate for the Multipurpose Arthritis Center in the Department of Medicine, Northwestern University Medical School, Chicago. He is a social psychologist and is adjunct faculty in the Department of Psychology at Loyola University Chicago.

The methodology of multiple sites in evaluation research requires a balance between benefits and challenges.

Multiple Sites in Evaluation Research: A Survey of Organizational and Methodological Issues

James M. Sinacore, Robin S. Turpin

During the past few years, investigators have shown a growing interest in evaluating programs that are implemented at multiple sites. This trend is not surprising because such evaluations can have considerable benefits. For example, the use of multiple sites, in increasing the size of samples, elevates the statistical power of analyses and hence the validity and reliability of findings. This advantage has especially practical consequences for programs that are designed for a highly technical or specialized audience, such as orthopedic surgeons learning how to perform a new type of joint replacement. Evaluation of programs at multiple locations is also advantageous when it is important to generalize program effects across a diverse range of individuals, such as those in need of job-finding skills.

Despite the variety of reasons for using multiple sites, there is no available source for one to learn about this approach to evaluation. In this chapter, we thus discuss the issues that face investigators who conduct multisite evaluations (MSEs). Our main contention is that a MSE, like any other methodology, has benefits and challenges that must be weighed and balanced. Evaluators must be cognizant of these elements and decide to conduct a MSE only when they conclude that the advantages outweigh the limitations of this approach.

This chapter is organized into seven main sections. First, we offer a definition of MSEs. Second, we discuss how MSEs can enhance the generalizability of program findings. We then review, third, various topics on the administration of MSEs and, fourth, issues involving cross-site communication and other social factors. Next, we address issues of, fifth, data quality control and, sixth, statistical analysis. Seventh, the chapter closes with final considerations and a brief conclusion.

Although each of these areas can be discussed in depth, we have opted to provide readers with an overview for two reasons. First, it is impossible to offer a detailed discussion in the allotted space for this chapter. Second (and of greater importance), we want readers to see the "big picture" of MSEs, that is, our aim is to inform evaluators about what they need to consider for an MSE rather than to describe how to solve specific problems.

Definition of a Multisite Evaluation

At present, there are no established criteria for defining an MSE. However, our observation of current practices indicates that these evaluations can be classified into two main categories: prospective and retrospective. A prospective MSE is one in which an investigator intends to use multiple sites at the beginning of an evaluation. In our opinion, a prospective MSE is the more productive of the two types because an evaluator works on the project from inception and thus has the time to anticipate difficulties and implement corrective measures.

A retrospective MSE is one in which the data from different evaluations on a similar topic are brought together for an analysis. Here, the use of multiple sites is an afterthought. Although the practice is probably not too common, this type of MSE is performed when two or more evaluators become aware of each other's work and believe that the combination or the comparison of data from individual projects will strengthen their understanding of the programs under study. Of course, additional care needs to be exercised with a retrospective MSE because it poses significant problems (such as dissimilar program participants) that are not easily corrected.

Whether prospective or retrospective in nature, MSEs are usually organized in two ways. One subtype of MSE is an evaluation of a program that is implemented *in the same way* at different geographical locations. An example of this is an evaluation of a prenatal care program offered to unwed mothers who live in different parts of a large metropolitan city. Following data collection, evaluators combine the data from all sites to test the impact of the program on participants' knowledge and skills. In Chapter Two of this volume, Susan C. Hedrick and her colleagues provide an in-depth example of this kind of MSE. MSEs of this type are similar to multicenter clinical trials (also known as cooperative studies) conducted by medical or public health investigators (Alamercery, Wilkins, Karrison, and IMPACT Research Group, 1986; Gaston and others, 1987; Meinert, 1988; "Organization, Review, and Administration . . . ," 1988).

Another subtype of MSE is an evaluation of a program that is implemented *in different ways* at different geographical locations. An example of this is an evaluation that examines different instructional methods to educate nurses about new developments in the treatment of rheumatoid arthritis. One site uses a teacher-centered method (lectures), another uses a student-centered method (independent readings), and a third uses a Socratic method (interactive questions and answers). This approach is somewhat problematical because location and program format are confounded. If there are observed differences in outcomes among the sites, it is not clear whether those differences are caused by the various program formats or by the unique features of the sites in which the programs are provided (for example, the style in which program personnel interact with program recipients might foster outcome differences). However, this subtype of MSE might be the only realistic way in which an evaluator can compare the efficacy of different program formats. In Chapter Three of this volume, Albert J. Reiss, Jr., and Robert Boruch describe the Spouse Assault Replication Program, which is an example of this type of MSE in the criminal justice area.

The distinguishing feature of an MSE is its implementation at different sites with an analysis of *original* data. MSEs should not be confused with metanalyses in which investigators study the effects of programs by examining the summary statistics of numerous published and unpublished evaluations (see Light and Pillemer, 1984).

Generalizability

One of the main benefits of an MSE is that it can facilitate the generalizability of findings. This factor is referred to as external validity (Cook and Campbell, 1979). By its very nature, the collection of data from multiple sites can aid in determining the extent to which a program influences different types of individuals.

Textbooks on research and survey methodology note that generalizability is best when the participants of a study have been chosen randomly from a known population (for example, see Sudman, 1976). When conducting an evaluation, however, random sampling is not always feasible, nor is it usually desired by major stakeholders. In such cases, Cook and Campbell (1979) suggest that *deliberate sampling for heterogeneity* helps increase external validity. This is achieved by selecting individuals who represent a range of desired target classes of people—a task that can be accomplished with multiple sites. For example, an evaluator who is interested in examining a new reading program might be concerned that it will be differentially efficacious among children from families of different socioeconomic backgrounds (because the families presumably differ on the values that parents place on reading). If stratified sampling is not possible, the evaluator could examine children in different socioeconomic environments by implementing the reading program in different grade schools, for example, one school in the inner-city, another in a middle-class suburb, and still another in an affluent suburb. If the children who receive the program are found to read better than those who do not, it would suggest that the program has observable effects despite socioeconomic differences among the children.

Statistically speaking, deliberate sampling for heterogeneity does not allow one to generalize in meaningful ways to a larger population. This is because selection is not random. However, the variation in participants that is created by using multiple sites allows the evaluator to examine the extent to which a program influences different types of people. For example, if it were shown that the reading program in question was successful at all the sites, it would be known that children across three socioeconomic levels were affected by the program. Given this outcome, something would be learned about the efficacy of the program relative to specific groups of different socioeconomic levels. It would not be known if the same results would be found with a stratified random sample, but at least it can be said that an effect was obtained across the particular range of children involved in the evaluation.

Evaluators should be careful. If they create too much discrepancy among participants at different sites, they increase the likelihood of a program-by-site interaction (that is, an inconsistency in the difference between group means across program sites). This factor interaction interferes with the ability to combine the sites for an overall analysis. Consequently, an analysis must be conducted separately for each site. For example, if an MSE of an alcohol rehabilitation program is conducted with American Indians at one site and Hispanic migrant workers at another, it might be difficult, if not impossible, to combine the two sites for a joint analysis of program effects. The cultural differences between the sites could predispose participants to respond to the same program in very different ways.

Administrative Issues

There are several key administrative issues that must be considered when contemplating a program evaluation, including staffing, training collaboration of program providers, and cost. Using multiple sites to conduct the evaluation adds an additional layer of complication to this decision-making process.

Staffing Plans. Developing a functional staffing plan must be one of the first considerations, and this will have an important effect on data quality. The approach that is taken depends on budget, time commitment from each site, personal motivation and enthusiasm for the project, and the authority that can be exercised over each site.

The approach that takes the least expenditure in dollars and in hiring and training effort involves the use of existing staff as site coordinators and data collectors. However, this can only occur when the evaluator (or the authority behind the evaluator) has influence over the personnel at each site. For example, public funding sources frequently require a minimum percentage of program dollars to be spent on evaluation. Under this circumstance, program providers have a motivation to participate in the study. By devoting a percentage of staff time to the evaluation, an organization is able to fulfill this funding requirement. A similar situation occurs when providers must conduct research to advance in their careers. This is frequently a requirement of provider or service organizations as well as of professional associations. For example, many health care organizations require nursing staff to participate in research in order to be promoted to management levels, which results in greater personal motivation for participation.

If there is no motivation present, there must be some enthusiasm and commitment that leads program providers to voluntarily participate in the project. Participation of this kind can be difficult to achieve because providers are frequently understaffed and may be unable to assume another task. Yet, even this disadvantage can be overcome if the evaluator is able to inspire the providers with perceived benefits to both their clients and themselves. In one evaluation, we were able to convince social workers at eighteen hospitals that the time they would spend on data collection would help them to better understand their spinal-cord-injured patients. At the end of the study, each social worker received copies of the final report describing the entire study, and of a special report profiling the patients at their respective facilities.

Another approach is to actually hire research staff at each site. Naturally, this strategy requires a substantial budget, but it might be the only reasonable solution if data collection entails considerable effort or if site resources are constrained. Studies with substantial budgets are typically found in multisite clinical trials in which drugs or surgical and medical procedures are evaluated.

A third approach is to have all staff centrally located, whereby personnel travel to the various sites to collect data. This is efficient if the sites are in close proximity or if the data collection can take place over a short period so that the work at each site can be staggered. Otherwise, extended travel results in increased costs and staff retention problems.

Training. Once staffing need are identified and personnel are in place, training becomes the next issue. Like staffing, training depends on the budget. A group conference is frequently the most efficient means of achieving high-quality training. On occasion, these types of sessions can be held in conjunction with national association meetings to minimize costs (however, the training of individuals with limited research experience might require a more intensive approach). Training manuals distributed prior to the group conference are important to ensuring the collection of high-quality data. A less expensive option may be for a trainer to travel to each site as necessary.

If travel funds are limited, the training manuals become vital to maximizing uniformity in data collection. In this situation, access to other means of communication, such as conference calls for purposes of training or problem solving, and the immediate availability of the phone or fax to evaluators, trainers, and other problem solvers throughout the study are essential.

Selection of Site Collaborators. The selection of collaborators to supervise staff and data collection is another important and sometimes complicated issue. The presence of a coordinator or coinvestigator at each site allows for the efficient handling of everyday organizational problems, needs, and decisions. Successful studies are frequently organized so that each site has an individual, located fairly high within the organization, who serves in this capacity. These individuals either can have a limited involvement in the development of the study or can serve as full coinvestigators with a more significant role. The latter often receive prominence in publications as well. Those with less involvement may be authors on secondary papers or may not be listed on any publication, but their contributions certainly should be acknowledged.

Cost. One particularly attractive benefit of MSEs is that more data can be collected over a shorter length of time than is possible with a single-site study. This benefit often results in the formulation of studies that are larger than one otherwise would have planned.

The move to multiple sites can result in more efficient expenditures of both fixed and variable costs, including office rent and salaries. However, on occasion there can be a decrease in efficiency in these expenditures, for example, when offices must be rented and furnished and staff hired at each site, even if the study work load at each of these sites is not heavy. Thus, an MSE could cost more for data collection per site than would a single-site study, although the cost per subject would probably decrease. On the other hand, the availability of extra personnel support can be a powerful incentive for a site to participate.

There are some costs that inevitably increase when MSEs are used for a study. Depending on staffing patterns, travel costs can rise, sometimes significantly. There will also be increases in phone and mail costs. Overhead costs, such as support staff, also expand. And more support is needed to plan the additional travel and site coordination.

Overall, whether an MSE is more or less expensive than a single-site study depends on individual circumstances. Once staffing decisions are made, other expenses depend on the coordination needs of the study headquarters and of the individual sites.

Cross-Site Communication and Other Social Issues

Although awareness of various communication or social obstacles is essential in conducting any program evaluation, this need is intensified when planning MSEs. Thus, considerations of the applicable stakeholders, and diverse political climates and cultural differences, can be key to the successful and timely completion of MSEs.

Stakeholders' Benefits. One particularly gratifying benefit of MSEs is that, if planned and executed properly, ownership of the programs or interventions is nurtured at the sites. The stakeholders feel that they have not merely been subjected to the results of an outside evaluation. This sense of stakeholder involvement is important, especially when the evaluation is not expected to be well received, because the research sites of an MSE typically do not include the "home base" of the study. By actively participating in the MSE, personnel have a stake in producing a high-quality product.

Political Climate. One area that has strong ramifications for the success or failure of an MSE encompasses social and communication issues. While most of us are aware of the political aspects of evaluation research, the multiple political environments of an MSE can be easily overlooked. Even if there is a strong central figure for the study who has influence over participation, there are frequently gatekeepers at each site who can influence data quality. Therefore, it is imperative for evaluators to become aware of the political climate at each site and to respond accordingly.

Cultural Differences. In a similar vein, the different cultures and traditions of research sites, including not only cultural differences of the people who live in each region but also traditions within the organizations, may result in organizational difficulties for the study. For example, differences in pace of living and working habits may have serious consequences for a multisite study, particularly one that is on a tight time schedule. Local organizational traditions, such as independence from a centralized authority, may also have important effects.

In sum, a high-quality MSE depends on the evaluator's knowledge about the sites—their organizations and personnel—before including them in the study. A common wisdom in the Department of Veterans Affairs states, "When you have seen one VA, you have seen one VA." This message should be well heeded. The wise evaluator verifies any claims regarding similarity of prospective sites while planning an MSE.

Quality Control

Expanding a study to include multiple sites poses a special challenge to maintaining control over the quality of the data. Subsequently, special factors are involved in the efficiency and standardization of data collection, organization, and verification that must be considered.

Efficiency of Data Collection. One of the best reasons for conducting MSEs is the efficiency with which data can be collected. Depending on the autonomy of the sites, data also can be entered into the central computer and edited quickly and efficiently.

Standardization of Data Collection. Standardization of at least some of the scientific and organizational instruments and procedures is absolutely key to a successful MSE. The end result is an evaluation of a program prototype across sites. For some MSEs, complete standardization is desirable and necessary (see Hedrick and others, this volume).

If local adaptation of the program is necessary, additional data can be collected to reflect the unique aspects of the sites (see Mowbray and Herman, and Cottingham, this volume). Consequently, this two-stage evaluation may consist of standardized instruments to evaluate the prototype and additional, perhaps more open-ended, instruments to evaluate local adaptations.

While use of the same instruments across sites is easier than the use of different instruments, actual implementation of the standardized instruments can also vary widely, even when data collectors have been adequately trained.

Standardization of Data Organization. Standardization across sites involves more than data collection. It also includes data organization and storage, computer entry, and editing. If these tasks are performed at a central site, standardization will be a minor issue. This decision depends on the project staff. When data are organized, filed, stored, computerized, and edited at each site, it is imperative that the individuals assigned to these tasks receive adequate training, and that each follows the same procedures using compatible equipment. The need for this meticulous care quickly becomes apparent when the data collection sites are contacted for information. No matter how well planned, it is inevitable that some of the data submitted by the sites are incomplete, confusing, or erroneous. There is a need to plan for verification; consequently, standardization of procedures becomes essential, especially if there is staff turnover. If all data are organized on paper and in computer files in an identical manner, anyone connected with the project should be able to retrieve the necessary information.

Data Verification. A final aspect of quality control is the use of data auditing and verification. Many evaluators have found these procedures to be very helpful in measuring the quality of data collection, both during the project and afterward. An audit can take many forms, from computerized checks of data for responses outside the expected range, to random checks of data for accuracy and completeness. If the audit occurs during the project, sites with unusually high error rates can be identified and the problems rectified. If the audit must be delayed until the study is complete, it can give evaluators confidence in the quality of data, as well as convince others of the legitimacy and quality of the evaluation.

Statistical Analysis

Analysis of data from an MSE poses concerns that typically do not confront the evaluator who examines a program at a single site. Although no one has yet fully discussed analytic concerns, Fleiss (1986) has addressed related statistical issues in the context of multicenter clinical trials.

In the present section we discuss issues that are of central importance to the analysis of data from an MSE and present recommendations in order to help evaluators think more clearly about their analytical strategies.

Analysis Plan. In planning an MSE, evaluators should think about how the data will be analyzed. For example, if the same program will be implemented at different locations, one has to decide if the program effects should be analyzed on a site-by-site basis or if the data can be "pooled" in order to test for an overall effect.

When considering an analysis plan, evaluators should not overlook the fact that the sites will vary from one another in overall mean responses to the program. In other words, sites will vary in the differences exhibited between the treatment and comparison groups. This variance can be attributed to two factors: (1) differences in demographics and needs for program services among the participants and (2) differences in program implementation. Although both factors are analytical nuisances, it is the second that is more likely to produce a program-by-site interaction. This is because differences in program implementation are typically stable and thus introduce a *systematic* influence on participants. Differences in demographics and need are usually variable and, more often than not, introduce a form of *random* variation. (Differences in demographics can also produce program-by-site interactions, but this does not occur very often. However, see the prior section on generalizability for an example.)

When a program-by-site interaction is present, it is not prudent to combine the data from all of the sites because the difference in means of the treatment and comparison groups will not be interpretable. This could lead the evaluator to overlook important program effects that occur at a particular site. However, evaluators are usually interested in pooling data across sites. Therefore, it is important to understand the ways in which pooling can be conducted as well as the related consequences. Moreover, evaluators should plan for the possibility of detecting a program-by-site interaction so that the pooling of data will not hinder proper interpretation of results.

Pooling Data. Data are pooled across sites in order to find an overall program effect. There are, however, two ways in which the pooling can be achieved (Fleiss, 1986). First, data can be pooled by averaging within-site differences. This means that the effect of a program is assessed at each site and then the effects are averaged across the sites. We call this *pooling by averaging.* This is similar to what happens when one pools variance for statistical computations. Second, data can be pooled simply by adding together all of the data from people in a similar treatment group, irrespective of site. When this is done, the effect of a program is assessed as though the data originated from one location. We call this *pooling by lumping.*

At the outset, the difference between these types of pooling might seem trivial. However, Fleiss (1986) notes that each has its appropriate use. Pooling by averaging is correct when participants are assigned to treatment groups within each site, independently of the other sites. In this case, the method of pooling is determined by research design. Pooling by lumping is theoretically appropriate only when participants can be assigned to a treatment group, irrespective of site, so that it is possible for most or all of the participants at one location to receive the same treatment. Although such an assignment strategy is unusual, it has been employed in multiclinic cancer trials in which stratification by stage of disease was considered more important than the control of clinic variation (Lagakos and Pocock, 1984; Lange and MacIntyre, 1985; Pocock and Lagakos, 1982).

The two methods of pooling have statistical consequences. A positive feature of both is that the difference among group means will be an unbiased estimator of the difference in population means, assuming that there is no program-by-site interaction. However, the sampling variation of the difference in group means will typically be greater for pooling by lumping. This is because the variation is influenced by differences among the sites that are always assumed to be present (Fleiss, 1986). Larger sample sizes are therefore needed to compensate for the inflation of variance in order to preserve adequate statistical power.

In theory, pooling by averaging is appropriate for the MSE because assignment to treatment groups is typically made within sites. This method is not practical, however, because standard statistical equations need to be modified to account for this form of pooling. Such modifications are not available to evaluators outside of an occasional technical research article.

Given our observation of current practices, most MSEs pool data by lumping. However, everyone needs to understand that by simply amassing data from all of the sites into one analysis, a major statistical challenge arises. It is therefore recommended that evaluators conduct a realistic analysis of statistical power with multisite pilot data. This pilot run should lead to sample sizes that are large enough to overcome the statistical "noise" generated by lumping.

Detecting a Program-by-Site Interaction. When an MSE is conducted, it is generally not known if a program-by-site interaction is present. If all goes well, this factor interaction will not occur. However, we recommend that evaluators look for this type of interaction in order to see if an overall analysis is going to be interpretable.

One way of looking for this interaction is to view site and treatment group as two factors in an analysis-of-variance (ANOVA) framework. Although this might seem like a complicated approach, it is not difficult if the original design of the evaluation is kept simple. For example, assume that a cardiac rehabilitation program has been implemented at three hospitals. Within each location the evaluators have randomly assigned recent heart attack patients either to participate in the program or to continue with customary care. Assume further that the main outcome variable is psychological well-being.

With two treatment groups (the program versus customary care) and three sites, participants' well-being scores can be analyzed with a two-by-three ANOVA. Within this analysis a program-by-site interaction can be tested statistically. (Technically, this should be called a *treatment*-by-site interaction because cardiac program and customary care reflect two levels of a treatment factor. However, the interaction is referred to here as *program*-by-site for consistency with the earlier discussion.) The interaction will not be significant if the participants have responded to the program in a similar way at each of the hospitals. In this case, the sites can be combined for an overall analysis. In fact, one could simply examine the main effect for treatment, which tests for a difference in well-being between the program and comparison groups, disregarding site. In contrast, the interaction will be significant if the participants have responded differently in at least one of the locations. When this occurs, it will be necessary to examine the results of each site to see if some of the sites can be combined.

Figure 1 depicts one type of a program-by-site interaction that could be found in our hypothetical MSE of a cardiac rehabilitation program. In this figure, the mean well-being scores of both treatment groups are plotted as a function of site. Visual inspection clearly shows that people in the program are doing better than those who were assigned to customary care, irrespective of site. However, the *degree* of impact of the program appears to be similar for sites A and C and disproportionately large for site B. Given these results, it would be reasonable to combine sites A and C for an analysis. Site B should be analyzed separately.

The results shown in Figure 1 are relatively clear. Such clarity of results will not always be achieved. If a program-by-site interaction is found and sites cannot easily be grouped visually, effect sizes can be computed for each site. This method provides a numerical index by which the sites can be grouped. Because effect-size computations are related to design, a discussion of equations is beyond the scope of this chapter. (For effect-size equations that are applicable to a variety of situations, see Cohen, 1988; Lipsey, 1990).

It is important to determine the reason for a program-by-site interaction. In our hypothetical MSE above, the outcome for site B could be different for a number of reasons. For example, the program might have been implemented there in a way that is different from the other two sites, or else the participants at site B might have been the least debilitated. In either case, an explanation of the interaction typically helps to put findings into perspective.

The use of an ANOVA model will not help in detection of program-by-site interactions in all cases. We nonetheless recommend that evaluators

**Figure 1. Program-by-Site Interaction in a
Hypothetical Multisite Evaluation**

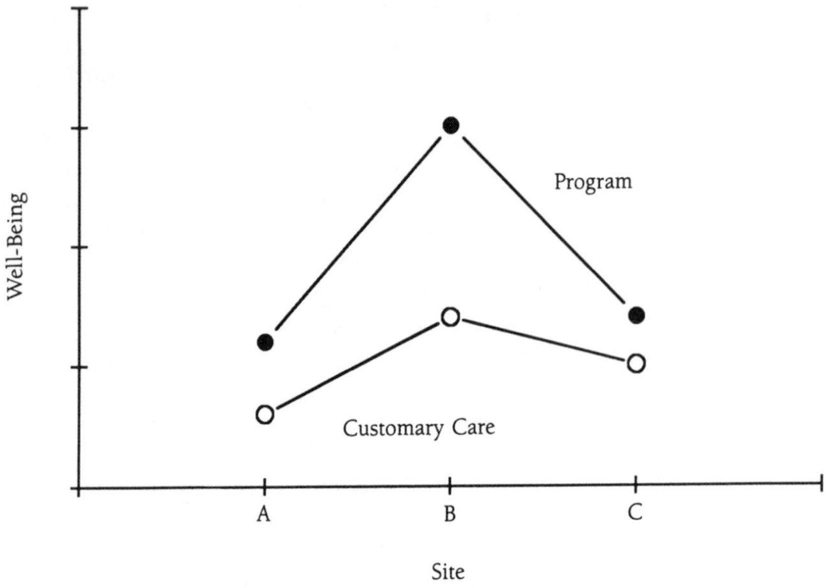

Note: In this hypothetical evaluation of a cardiac rehabilitation program, a two-by-three analysis of variance is employed. There are two treatment groups (program versus customary care) and three sites (hospitals). The main dependent variable is the psychological well-being of the patients.

take the time to explore the results of each site *in some way* before lumping them together. Any attempt to look at site differences is better than indiscriminate lumping of all of the sites into one analysis. In the long run, this extra caution will help reduce erroneous conclusions.

In summary, we realize that our discussion of statistical issues cannot provide guidance on all problems for all situations. However, we have presented some of the major analytical concerns encountered in MSEs.

Final Considerations

The decision to use multiple sites in an evaluation has consequences not only for the study but also for the evaluator. In weighing the benefits and challenges of an MSE, the abilities, preferences, and personality of the evaluator play an important role. The evaluator may be well aware that there are multiple political climates and personalities that require diplomatic management, yet he or she may not have the desire or inclination to d̶e̶a̶l̶ with these issues. It may also be outside the experience or preferen the evaluator to deal with the sometimes frustrating and complex organizational aspects of an MSE. Thus, the evaluator may opt for a single site. While the MSE does have some important advantages, its administrative and organizational complications can increase the frustration involved in conducting an evaluation. Thus, the decision to conduct an evaluation at multiple sites is related to professional as well as personal concerns.

Conclusion

In this chapter we have provided an overview of the organizational and methodological issues germane to MSEs. Following a conceptualization of MSEs, we discussed the topics of generalizability, administration, communication among the sites, data quality control, and statistical analysis. We have surveyed these issues in order to nurture a general appreciation of this area of professional evaluation.

From this presentation we want evaluators to understand that the choice of an MSE should be based on a careful weighing of advantages and limitations of the method. For example, MSEs facilitate generalization and can provide large sample sizes, yet they sometimes require additional personnel and always require special organizational and communication skills. Thus, if an evaluator desires the benefits but does not want to, or is unable to, deal with the challenges, then an MSE should not be considered. However, if an evaluator views the challenges as an opportunity to exercise his or her research skills, then an MSE is probably in order.

Use of MSEs is slowly on the rise. Indeed, some evaluators are presently conducting MSEs without realizing that the techniques involved are emerging as a new area of methodological expertise in professional evaluation. Therefore, evaluators who are aware of the advantages and the demands of MSEs will be prepared to conduct the best evaluations of this type. As interest in MSEs continues to grow over the next few years, we expect that many evaluators will come to recognize the potentially rich data sets that MSEs can offer.

References

Alamercery, Y., Wilkins, P., Karrison, T., and IMPACT Research Group. "Functional Equality of Coordinating Centers in a Multicenter Clinical Trial: Experience of the International Mexiletine and Placebo Anti-Arrhythmic Coronary Trial (IMPACT)." *Controlled Clinical Trials*, 1986, 7 (1), 38–51.

Cohen, J. *Statistical Power Analysis for the Behavioral Sciences*. (2nd ed.) Hillsdale, N.J.: Erlbaum, 1988.

Cook, T. D., and Campbell, D. T. *Quasi-Experimentation: Design and Analysis Issues for Field Settings*. Boston: Houghton Mifflin, 1979.

Fleiss, J. L. "Analysis of Data from Multiclinic Trials." *Controlled Clinical Trials*, 1986, 7 (4), 267–275.

Gaston, M., Smith, J., Gallagher, D., Flournoy-Gill, Z., West, S., Bellevue, R., Farber, M., Grover, R., Koshy, M., Ritchey, A. K., Wilimas, J., Verter, J., and CSSCD Study Group. "Recruitment in the Cooperative Study of Sickle Cell Disease (CSSCD)." *Controlled Clinical Trials*, 1987, *8* (4), 131S–140S.

Lagakos, S. W., and Pocock, S. J. "Randomization and Stratification in Cancer Clinical Trials: An International Perspective." In M. E. Buyse, M. J. Staquet, and R. J. Sylvester (eds.), *Cancer Clinical Trials: Methods and Practice*. Oxford, England: Oxford University Press, 1984.

Lange, N., and MacIntyre, J. "A Computerized Patient Registration and Treatment Randomization System for Multi-Institutional Clinical Trials." *Controlled Clinical Trials*, 1985, *6* (1), 38–50.

Light, R. J., and Pillemer, D. B. *Summing Up: The Science of Reviewing Research*. Cambridge, Mass.: Harvard University Press, 1984.

Lipsey, M. W. *Design Sensitivity: Statistical Power for Experimental Research*. Newbury Park, Calif.: Sage, 1990.

Meinert, C. L. "NIH Multicenter Investigator-Initiated Trials: An Endangered Species?" *Controlled Clinical Trials*, 1988, *9* (2), 97–102.

"Organization, Review, and Administration of Cooperative Studies (Greenberg Report): A Report from the Heart Special Project Committee to the National Advisory Heart Council, May 1967." *Controlled Clinical Trials*, 1988, *9* (2), 137–148.

Pocock, S. J., and Lagakos, S. W. "Practical Experience of Randomization in Cancer Trials: An International Survey." *British Journal of Cancer*, 1982, *46* (3), 368–375.

Sudman, S. *Applied Sampling*. San Diego, Calif.: Academic Press, 1976.

James M. Sinacore is statistician and research associate for the Multipurpose Arthritis Center in the Department of Medicine, Northwestern University Medical School, Chicago. He is a social psychologist and is adjunct faculty in the Department of Psychology at Loyola University Chicago.

Robin S. Turpin is senior coordinator, Research and Sponsored Programs, for Lutheran General Health Care System in Park Ridge, Illinois. She was formerly senior health scientist at the Health Services Research and Development Field Program of Hines Veterans Administration Hospital. She is a social psychologist and is adjunct faculty in the Department of Psychology, Loyola University Chicago.

Decisions about the appropriate balance between centralized and decentralized staffing and responsibilities in multisite evaluations should be based on scientific, administrative, and political considerations.

Centralized Versus Decentralized Coordination in the Adult Day Health Care Evaluation Study

Susan C. Hedrick, Jean H. Sullivan, Jenifer L. Ehreth, Margaret L. Rothman, Richard T. Connis, William W. Erdly

This chapter describes the approaches to multisite coordination developed during the three years of pilot funding and three years of operation of the Adult Day Health Care Evaluation Study. Our focus is on the task of achieving the appropriate balance between centralized versus decentralized staffing and direction. We begin with a brief overview of our study and a discussion of the importance of understanding the evaluation setting. We then discuss study support, site staff issues, and various issues unique to the procedures of collecting data on cost of health care services.

Study Overview

In 1983, Congress authorized the Veterans Administration, now the Department of Veterans Affairs (DVA), to provide Adult Day Health Care (ADHC): "a therapeutically oriented ambulatory day program which provides health maintenance and rehabilitative services to frail elderly individuals in a congregate setting during daytime hours" (Veterans Administration, 1987, p. 1). Interest in information about this promising but relatively untested

This research was supported by the Department of Veterans Affairs Health Services Research and Development Service, Project #SDR 85-07. The opinions expressed are those of the authors and do not necessarily reflect the views of the Department of Veterans Affairs.

program led Congress to mandate in the same legislation "a study of the medical efficacy and cost effectiveness of furnishing such care" (U.S. Congress, 1983, p. B4). The ADHC Evaluation Study discussed here is the result of that mandate. We conducted the study at eight DVA medical centers in two phases: Phase 1 was a randomized, controlled trial of ADHC provided directly by the DVA at the four sites of Little Rock, Arkansas; Miami, Florida; Minneapolis, Minnesota; and Portland, Oregon. Phase 2 was a nonrandomized, prospective study of ADHC provided under contract to DVA at the four additional sites of Chicago, Illinois; Phoenix, Arizona; San Diego, California; and Seattle/Tacoma, Washington. The methodology is described in Hedrick and others (1991).

The factors that necessitated a multicenter study were (1) a congressional mandate to compare the two types of ADHC, which could not both be offered at one site, (2) the importance of findings that could be generalized across all 172 DVA medical centers, (3) the interest in assessing differences among all eight ADHC programs and their association with program outcomes, and (4) the interest in assessing the differential effects of ADHC for various subgroups of patients (for example, older versus younger, or more or less impaired at intake), which required a large number of patients for sufficient statistical power.

Our approach to multisite study coordination involved a strong degree of centralized control. Full-time staff at the central office included the principal investigator, co-investigators, project director, field staff coordinators, data entry and data management staff, research assistants, administrative assistant, and secretary. Our approach also involved strong local direction. Site staff included a professional-level site coordinator (usually with a Ph.D. or M.D. degree), casefinders who recruited and screened patients for the study (registered nurses or social workers), interviewers, a cost data collector, and a secretary. Data entry, management, and analysis were conducted at the central office. Most other activities were conducted jointly by the central office and on-site staff.

We based our decisions about the appropriate balance between centralized and decentralized staffing and responsibilities on scientific, administrative, and political factors in our analysis of the necessary tasks to be accomplished. The four task areas discussed here are the securing of interest in and cooperation for our study from site staff, casefinding, in-person data collection, and record extraction on the cost and utilization of health care services.

Understanding the System

Our first step in designing this study was to gain a thorough understanding of the advantages and constraints of working within the DVA system. DVA has a long history of conducting multicenter randomized trials on biomedical topics. As the largest health care system in the nation, DVA's success in this endeavor owes much to its relatively tight administrative structure (Remington, 1978) in which a "relatively high degree of medical, scientific and administrative control can be exercised" (James, 1980, p. 198). The opportunity to conduct a study in an organized system such as DVA did allow us a much greater degree of standardization than would have been possible in a group of unconnected hospitals with different procedures in such areas as staff hiring and supervision, medical and administrative records, and patient treatment. There remained, however, many differences in procedures across the eight sites with which we had to contend.

As one example of site-to-site differences, in the absence of a federal classification standard for a research interviewer, we developed a position description that was classified at one site and distributed to the others. The personnel departments at several other sites refused to follow the classification and requirements for experience and training, resulting in months of negotiation, delays in hiring interviewers with the necessary qualifications, and disparities in interviewer experience, salaries, and benefits. If we had discovered these differences earlier, we could have implemented sooner the procedures that were eventually followed, including an advisory review of the position description by personnel staff at DVA's Washington, D.C., central office, the use of interviewers with temporary status until regular positions were available, and formal agreements to adhere to centrally developed position descriptions as a condition of study participation.

Obtaining Cooperation

We combined centralized and decentralized approaches to obtaining cooperation from the site staff working on the study and from other staff at all levels of the organization. The study investigators took necessary initial actions such as securing the involvement of the staff responsible for the ADHC clinical programs at VA's central office in Washington, D.C. Among many other benefits, this procedure allowed participation in this study to be a condition of a medical center's designation as a clinical site. Other helpful strategies were the principal investigator's in-person meetings or telephone conversations at various times during study implementation with the directors and chiefs of staff of the medical centers. We also requested that the regional directors send a letter to each medical center asking for cooperation in patient recruitment and study implementation. Strong support from top-level administration in the organization, communication of study progress, and acknowledgments of the organization's contribution in interviews and publications can all be helpful in obtaining cooperation from personnel.

In our decentralized approach, the site coordinators represented our interests at each institution on an ongoing basis. We found that administrative and research experience within DVA were crucial qualifications for this position. The site coordinators represented the study on the official advisory committees to the ADHC clinical programs, when such committees were named. They were responsible for establishing and supervising informed-consent procedures because the rules varied so extensively from site to site. Their involvement was especially important in relation to problems with other medical center departments (for example, nursing, social work, data processing, personnel). As site employees they provided the in-depth knowledge of unique local conditions needed to guide implementation of study procedures. For example, they provided required administrative support as the study staff's official supervisors at the local level, which included signing time cards, conducting performance appraisals, and arranging for space, supplies, and equipment such as beepers.

The site coordinators had many other commitments and the number of administrative tasks was large. While the site coordinators had overall responsibility at the site, it was often helpful when the coordinator appointed an administrative assistant to work directly with the project director at the central office. The project director needed well-developed problem-solving abilities and communication skills to function as a resource person and aid each site coordinator in overseeing administrative details at the site.

Opportunities to conduct or participate in the pilot studies and other study development activities, to conduct supplemental studies (that is, separate studies using the main study data base), to participate in publications, and to participate in meetings of the study steering committee were helpful in increasing the site coordinators' identification and cooperation with the study. Similarly, the occasions in which the casefinders and interviewers were brought to the central office for training and retraining sessions not only proved crucial to the enhancement of their skills, but also were instrumental in supporting their commitment to the project, identification with study goals, and morale during their several years of work at the sites.

Site Staff Issues

Our approach to managing site staff activities combined central and site staffing and direction. The site coordinators, while the official site supervisors, were part-time workers in our study and did not have the time, interest, or experience necessary to provide detailed, day-to-day management of casefinders and interviewers. We needed individuals with appropriate experience to standardize activities across sites through consistent methods of selection, training, supervision, and quality control. We therefore hired an interviewer coordinator and a casefinder coordinator at the central office who were responsible for staff management across sites. In this structure some tasks, including recruitment and supervision of personnel, were shared by the site coordinator and central office coordinators; other tasks, including training and quality control, were consolidated at the central office. The following sections detail these activities and illustrate our decisions and recommendations for other, similar studies.

Hiring Current Site Employees. We found advantages and disadvantages in hiring current site employees for study positions. One advantage was that by hiring jointly with other projects at the site, we could fill our part-time positions and the individual would have the benefits of full-time employment. One disadvantage was that staff who were employed on other projects faced divided loyalties and conflicts in setting priorities. For example, our clerical support staff were paid one-quarter time and our tasks did not fall at easily scheduled intervals. Those staff frequently had difficulty accomplishing our work in a timely manner.

A second advantage in hiring current employees was their knowledge of the DVA system. For example, casefinders had clear advantages in their knowledge of procedures such as the operation of discharge planning on the wards and in their friendships with other staff. We found that overworked clinicians on the wards often decided whether to make referrals as much on the basis of their desire to help the casefinders as on the basis of their perceptions of the appropriateness of the referrals. However, casefinders hired from outside the system who had efficient working styles and attractive personalities could often overcome the initial disadvantage of lack of familiarity with the system.

For site coordinators, DVA experience was crucial. The site coordinator who was not a DVA employee continuously encountered problems because of lack of knowledge and clout within the system.

Staff Selection and Training. In addition to the screening provided by the site coordinators as the people officially responsible for site hiring, the interviewer coordinator screened all interviewer applicants over the telephone in a manner designed to ensure standardized recruitment and evaluation of these applicants. This screening included having each applicant administer a mock interview of questions taken from the patient questionnaire with the interviewer coordinator as respondent. The interviewer coordinator gave scripted responses to test the applicant's skill and aptitude and provided feedback on mistakes to test how well the applicants corrected their errors and dealt with constructive criticism and stress.

The interviewer coordinator directed a total of seven interviewer-training sessions at the central office. The sessions varied in length from five to eight days, depending on the number of people in the session. Training followed a fairly standard format and, during a two-week period following the central office sessions, interviewers tape-recorded full practice interviews with DVA patients and caregivers who were not part of the study.

In a less-structured process, the site coordinators and casefinder coordinator jointly selected study casefinders. The casefinder coordinator directed an initial, three-day training session at the central office, which covered program-marketing strategies, patient screening, data collection, and informed-consent procedures. Two retraining sessions were held over the eighteen months of patient screening to reinforce the use of standard procedures and to solve problems regarding marketing strategies and relationships with each medical center's clinical staff and study personnel.

Financial Cost and Other Considerations in Staffing Decisions. Our staffing decision of whether to hire one full-time interviewer or two part-time interviewers per site was partly dependent on the availability of travel monies required to provide centralized, in-person training. This budgeting was a particular problem since travel monies are very restrictive in DVA.

We also considered other factors. First, standard practice is to hire part-time interviewers since most interviewing takes place during evenings and weekends, when respondents typically are available. The target population for our study, however, was to a large extent homebound, so we decided that this standard practice was not a limiting factor for us. Second, we were concerned about potential interviewer attrition, which would result in additional training and data collection problems. Given the two-year field period, we felt that a full-time position with benefits such as vacation and sick leave would be more likely to attract highly skilled interviewers and would help prevent attrition. Therefore, partly in order to decrease travel costs, and partly to attract and hold qualified interviewers, we decided to hire one full-time interviewer instead of two part-time interviewers per site.

From a budgetary perspective, this decision enabled us to cut the travel costs in half for initial training. We also budgeted enough additional travel money in the first six months to cover the cost of interim training for one person in the event of attrition. Once we fielded the study, two interviewers quit within the first three months. Additional work load stresses occurred at a third site where enrollment was higher than expected. While it would have been ideal to hire an additional interviewer there earlier than planned, we could not do so because we needed available travel monies to handle work at the sites without interviewers.

In retrospect, the cost of dealing with the loss of the two interviewers nearly balanced out what it would have initially cost to train two people at each site. It was true that a full-time job was more attractive to some interviewers; however, as discussed later, the role conflict that the interviewers experienced appeared to have a greater effect on full-time interviewers than on part-time interviewers, and even some of the part-time interviewers had problems maintaining their commitment to us. Our strongest recommendation is to remember that financial cost is only one of several factors to be considered and that researchers must carefully identify and weigh other study-specific factors, such as length of field period, potential attrition and associated problems, difficulty of data collection instruments, and available pool of applicants, before making staffing decisions.

Supervision. The interviewer coordinator weekly telephoned each interviewer to receive reports on productivity, time, and mileage, in addition to conducting ad hoc telephone contacts as needed. Biweekly conference calls were also held with all interviewers during phase 1 of the study, in lieu of regular staff meetings that would typically occur in research with only one site. The interviewers each logged the time spent on activities such as interviewing, editing, and traveling and reported mileage actually traveled. These logs were in addition to routine DVA procedures used to report time and mileage and were designed to keep both the interviewer coordinator and the site coordinator informed about interviewer activities.

We also developed a computerized tracking system to keep the central site staff informed of the progress of the study across all sites and to help manage the interviewer work load. On a weekly basis, the system generated (1) summary reports across sites, by site and by interviewer, which provided the central site staff with an overview of productivity, (2) lists by interviewers of cases that were due for completion, and (3) lists of completed questionnaires that had not yet been received at the central office. The interviewer coordinator used these lists as a basis for the interviewers' weekly production reports, and the interviewers used the lists to organize their work in a timely manner. By tracking the receipt of interviews reported as complete, we were able to identify a situation where one interviewer falsely reported having completed work and we were able to act in a timely manner to satisfactorily resolve the problem.

The major method of interviewer quality control was to edit reviews at the central office. All in-person interviews were tape-recorded. The interview-edit coordinator reviewed a sample of those tapes, compared them to the completed questionnaires, and provided regularly scheduled feedback to the interviewers, working with them to solve problems and correct mistakes. This review of tape-recorded interviews provided a means not only of ensuring consistency in fieldwork procedures across sites, by a route more cost-effective than actual field supervision, but also of maintaining high performance levels among the interviewers.

The casefinder coordinator conducted biweekly conference calls with all casefinders, followed by letters summarizing agreements on major issues, and an average of one ad hoc telephone contact per week per casefinder. She also provided weekly feedback to the casefinders and research coordinators on the number of patients located at each site, information that supported casefinder motivation. While there was extensive contact between the casefinder coordinator and the casefinders, there were no regularly scheduled individual report times, and the casefinders did not regularly report their hours and daily activities to the patient-recruitment coordinator. In future, similar studies, we would recommend such standardized reporting of casefinder activities to help the casefinder coordinator guide these activities.

Role Conflict. Study staff often encountered high degrees of role conflict in the implementation of our procedures. Casefinders and interviewers, for example, encountered a great deal of role strain as they attempted to maintain a neutral stance as researchers and to limit their interaction with respondents to that clearly defined role. The casefinders were trained as nurses or social workers, however, and were used to a "helping" role rather than a neutral research role. As research staff, they had to sell the study as well as the program to patients, caregivers, and medical center staff and then deal with emotional letdown when patients did not meet the admissions criteria or, at the phase 1 sites, were assigned to customary care rather than to ADHC.

The interviewers maintained frequent contact with the patients and caregivers for up to a year. They faced problems such as suicidal patients, neglect of the elderly, and urgent unmet needs. They had to go into respondents' homes and maintain rapport as they conducted lengthy interviews, and at the same time they had to convince respondents, and themselves, that they could not take any action concerning respondents' problems.

Casefinders and interviewers also developed strong feelings about how the ADHC clinical programs could be improved to better meet patients' needs. But they were not in roles where they could effect any changes or even communicate those feelings to the clinical staff.

At times, as a result of the situations described above, the interviewers and casefinders needed intense supervision and support. Sometimes it was important that such support be immediate and face to face. In those instances the site coordinator proved to be a valuable resource.

Role conflict was also generated by the tensions inherent to situations where roles are shared by both central office and site staff, as was the case in our supervisory structure. The site coordinators were officially accountable for the activities of the casefinders and interviewers but did not have complete control over and, in some instances, did not have detailed knowledge of those activities. The casefinder and interviewer coordinators were responsible for meeting the research goals but did not have final authority over casefinder and interviewer activities and were not at the sites to experience events firsthand. Interviewers and casefinders were not always certain who was responsible in any given situation or to whom they should listen if they received conflicting information.

The solution to this type of role conflict is communication. It begins with early clarification during the planning stages of how roles will be defined and why. All parties need to understand the decisions, what is expected of them, and what the guidelines are for the roles they are expected to play. Some of the steps we took to achieve clarification and communication included regularly scheduled as well as ad hoc telephone contacts with staff and detailed written manuals.

Communication. Our decisions about the most appropriate frequency and type of communication between the central and site staff were collectively the most important single factor determining our study's success. Too frequent or intrusive communication at the sites can interfere with the ability of the staff to complete their tasks, whereas too infrequent communication can allow the development of nonstandardized procedures and prevent timely discovery and correction of performance problems. We suggest a general strategy of frequent contact at the beginning of the study, with the frequency gradually tapering off as allowed by successful implementation of procedures and acceptable levels of performance per site.

A combination of regularly scheduled as well as ad hoc telephone contacts is important to ensure consistent oversight of activities and to provide emotional and logistic support when needed. Routinely scheduled calls between the casefinder coordinator and the research coordinators were especially useful in our study in dealing with role conflict. They served to clarify situations where there was disagreement regarding casefinder procedures or performance. We originally scheduled weekly conferences between the site coordinator and the interviewer coordinator as well. But due to time constraints, these conferences only occurred when there was a problem. Conference calls, in which all casefinders, for example, were included, were time consuming and cumbersome but extremely important. Conference calls allowed for general brainstorming and resolution of problems, the latter of which was easily accepted by all staff members because of their contributions to the development of solutions. The conference calls fostered continued identification with the project, improved morale, and encouraged additional contacts between interviewers or casefinders at different sites for mutual problem solving and moral support.

While we tried electronic mail to simplify routine communication and reduce expenditures for postage, problems with site staff's access to and familiarity with the equipment reduced its effectiveness. These problems should diminish in future studies as the use of electronic mail systems becomes more routine in many organizations.

We also attempted to clarify roles by developing handbooks for the site coordinators, casefinders, and interviewers, describing their roles and interactions, detailing procedures and guidelines about the tasks we expected them to accomplish, the expected flow of data and information between the sites and the central office, and the support they could expect from the central office. Although these handbooks were useful, we experienced a definite trade-off between the level of detail provided and the extent to which staff were willing to use them.

Data Collection on Health Care Costs

The translation of scientific questions concerning the cost and utilization of all health care services into a strategy for collecting reliable, valid data presented a number of distinct challenges. While some data were collected from patient interviews, most were collected through the organizations that provided health care services, that is, the DVA medical centers and private physicians and hospitals. Data collection on cost and utilization could take advantage of DVA's centralized systems as long as they were adequate for our needs. Where they were not adequate, site-specific protocols for data collection had to be developed.

Information on each patient's use of DVA services was available from the Decentralized Hospital Computer Program (DHCP), a computerized management information system with a standardized structure across sites. The cost of those DVA services were calculated from a standardized fiscal reporting format used by administrators at each site. Since this procedure allowed one data collection policy for all eight sites but required specialized personnel to collect, interpret, and monitor data quality, our strategy was to centralize this portion of the data collection as much as possible.

The reports available from the computer were designed for use by managers of clinical units. For instance, it was possible for a clinic manager to get a report on all patients that had appointments for a particular day, and for a laboratory technician to get a report on the results of a lab test on a particular patient, but no one could get a report listing all the services received by a particular patient over the course of a year. We thus had to write a program that could extract the data needed for our purposes. Although the information system employed was supposed to be standardized, some sites had made minor adaptations to their own systems that required us to modify our extraction program and test it at each site. We also needed to ensure that the quality of data entry was consistent across sites by comparing the computer data to the hard copy medical records. The site research assistants selected a sample of these medical records for comparison to the DHCP data. The few variables that proved to be unreliable (such as the date of death and ZIP code) were collected from other sources.

Our development of a program to extract a large amount of information about individuals created an issue of confidentiality. While it was possible to write the program in such a way that we could access the data from the central office, the medical center computer personnel at the sites were concerned that they would lose control over their data, allowing for possible breaches of confidentiality as the extraction program became widely used. To allay this concern, we wrote a program that could only be accessed at each site. A site research assistant was hired to run the extraction program collecting these data. This research assistant also collected utilization and cost data for certain services not on the computerized system and worked with the administrative personnel to collect cost information.

The collection of data on non-DVA utilization required us to contact all non-DVA providers (that is, hospitals, physicians, clinics) reported by the patients in the patient questionnaire for verification of the information. Since this task required specialized knowledge of medical billing procedures, we chose to collect these data at the central office. We sent a personalized letter and a signed consent form to each provider, monitored their responses, sent reminder letters, coded their responses for data entry, and compared subject responses to provider responses prior to building the analytic data base. The use of a central office research assistant for this purpose proved advantageous in that there were many tasks that could be routinized after we gained some experience interacting with the providers.

For data collection on the cost of the ADHC programs, DAV's standardized financial reporting system allowed for a common terminology across sites and for similar organizational structures. However, differences across sites required the development of site-specific cost questionnaires. For instance, even for those ADHC programs located in the medical centers, the housekeeping and administrative services provided to each program were similar, but the methods used in the financial reporting system to allocate the cost of those services to the programs were different across sites. To develop the cost questionnaire, a central office researcher visited each site and met with the appropriate departmental personnel to learn how costs were generated and reported.

Overall, the centralized nature of DVA provided easy access to reliable data, but some accommodations were made for site-specific variations. These variations did not become obvious until data collection strategies were being implemented and validated.

Discussion

We have presented here some of the approaches to multisite coordination developed for the ADHC Evaluation Study. After an overview of the study, we discussed the importance of understanding the system within which a study will operate in order to discover problems, especially site-to-site differences, early enough to develop realistic timetables and creative solutions. We then presented our attempts to achieve an appropriate balance between centralized and decentralized activity in three major tasks of the study: the securing of interest and cooperation from site staff, both those employed in the study and in other departments; selection, training, and supervision of casefinders and interviewers; and collection of data on costs.

The particular advantages of ADHC Evaluation Study in achieving multisite coordination included the organized system within which the study was conducted, the congressional mandate, the early involvement of high-level administrators and of a steering committee of national DVA and non-DVA researchers and clinicians with experience in ADHC or multisite trials, and the three-year period for a pilot study to test actual casefinding and data collection strategies in multiple sites. The particular challenges of the study included major site-to-site differences in administrative procedures and patient populations, lengthy and complex casefinding and data collection procedures applied to a sample of very frail subjects, and ever-changing fiscal and political pressures on the clinical programs being evaluated.

The general success of the study is evidenced in part by the fact that 993 patients were enrolled, all of whom met the study admissions criteria. The interrater reliability and internal consistency coefficients were consistently high across sites, indicating the high quality of the data collected. Only 10 percent of the enrolled patients declined further participation over the year of data collection, reportedly because of the burden of illness in most cases, and only four enrolled patients could not be located for later interviews. The percentage of patients dropping out of the study did not vary dramatically across sites, ranging from 6 percent to 13 percent. We hope that the lessons learned in this study assist other researchers, and us, in future MSEs.

References

Hedrick, S. C., Rothman, M. L., Chapko, M. K., Inui, T. S., Kelly, J., Ehreth, J. L., and ADHC Evaluation Development Group. "Adult Day Health Care Evaluation Study: Methodology and Implementation." *Health Services Research*, 1991, *25* (6), 935–960.

James, K. E. "A Model for the Development, Conduct, and Monitoring of Multicenter Clinical Trials in the Veterans Administration." *Controlled Clinical Trials*, 1980, *1*, 193–207.

Remington, R. D. "Design and Management of Large Multicenter Trials." *Annals of the New York Academy of Sciences*, 1978, *304*, 244–253.

U.S. Congress. House. P.L. 98-160. *Title 1. Veterans Administration Heath-Care Programs*. H.R. 2920. 98th Cong., 1st sess., November 21, 1983.

Veterans Administration. Office of Geriatrics and Extended Care. *Adult Day Health Care Program Direction/Operating Instructions*. Washington, D.C.: Veterans Administration, 1987.

Susan C. Hedrick is principal investigator of the ADHC Evaluation Study, research health scientist with the Health Services Research and Development (HSR&D) Field Program at the Seattle VA Medical Center, and research assistant professor, Department of Health Services, University of Washington, Seattle.

Jean H. Sullivan is field coordinator of the Study and Research Health Scientist Specialist, HSR&D Field Program, Seattle.

Jenifer Ehreth is co-investigator with the study and assistant professor, Department of Health Services, University of Washington, Seattle.

Margaret L. Rothman is co-investigator with the study, research health scientist with the HSR&D Field Program, and affiliate assistant professor, Department of Health Services, University of Washington, Seattle.

Richard T. Connis is project director of the study and research associate, Department of Health Services, University of Washington, Seattle.

William W. Erdly is data manager of the study and research health scientist with the HSR&D Field Program, Seattle.

Coordination and oversight of multisite experiments for evaluation of criminal and civil justice projects can be improved through a Program Review Team approach.

The Program Review Team Approach and Multisite Experiments: The Spouse Assault Replication Program

Albert J. Reiss, Jr., Robert Boruch

This chapter outlines a Program Review Team (PRT) approach to coordination, oversight, and quality control in multisite experiments. The context is criminal justice research. The primary vehicle for illustration is the Spouse Assault Replication Program (SARP), a series of experiments designed to evaluate the effects of alternative ways in which police handle domestic violence.

Although the context is specialized, the PRT approach proposed here is general. Consequently, examples are also taken from other areas.

This chapter is a preliminary report. Additional experience may reveal other benefits and problems. In what follows, SARP is described first. Each of the six sites in the program and their experiments differed in some respects and were similar in others. This variation across sites is described. The PRT is the administrative and policy vehicle created to oversee and coordinate the field replications. Its mission, composition, operations, and reporting protocol are also described here. In the final sections of this chapter we deal with issues, benefits, and shortcomings of the PRT approach.

Spouse Assault Replication Program

SARP is a set of randomized field experiments that were undertaken in six sites. The effort was supported by the National Institute of Justice (NIJ), a research institute of the U.S. Department of Justice.

At each site, the police department, usually in cooperation with academic researchers, conducted randomized field tests of alternative approaches to police handling of misdemeanor incidents of domestic violence. (Felony incidents of domestic violence were excluded from random assignment to the proposed treatments.) Until quite recently, the conventional police approach to such incidents was to mediate the dispute, occasionally separating the disputants. An alternative approach tested in all sites was arrest. That is, when probable cause for a misdemeanor offense was established, police could make an arrest instead of mediating domestic disputes or separating the disputants before moving on to the next call. (In one of the jurisdictions, Milwaukee, a city council ordinance mandated arrest. The council had to approve randomized assignment to exempt the police department from this mandated disposition.)

In the simplest case, police officers who were dispatched to a call determined whether a domestic violence case was eligible for the experiment. When eligibility was established, the case was *randomly* assigned to one of the two or more treatments being tested, for example, arrest versus mediation.

The "new treatment," arrest, was common to all six sites. This conforms to the NIJ's general program objective of determining whether the results of an earlier, important experiment in Minneapolis could be replicated (Sherman and Berk, 1984). That experiment's results suggested that there was a deterrent effect of the arrest treatment when compared with customary mediation and separation treatments, that is, there was significantly less repeat volume for the arrested men. But Minneapolis is sufficiently unique, relative to other jurisdictions, the original experiment sufficiently imperfect, and the policy issue sufficiently important to justify a program of replication experiments. Would arrest or some other treatments account for the greater reduction in recidivism?

SARP, therefore, involved testing one or more alternatives to arrest. This latitude was permitted, even encouraged by NIJ, to get beyond simplistic notions of replication and to maximize the experiments' benefits, notably evidence for policy and science, relative to costs. In Omaha, for instance, alleged offenders who were "gone on arrival" (that is, who had fled the scene) were randomly allocated to an "issuance of a warrant" treatment, a warrant that could lead to subsequent arrest if the spouse failed to appear in court (Dunford, Huizinga, and Elliott, 1990). In Milwaukee, police employed an arrest dosage treatment. Eligible cases were randomly assigned to an Arrest-and-Hold treatment (usually eight hours), to an Arrest-and-Release treatment (usually within two hours), or to a Warning treatment without an arrest.

The SARP experiments were directed by different principal investigators (PIs). The PIs were academic researchers, experts in criminal justice research with strong ties to local police departments, or police department employees. The six sites and the principal investigators were (1) Atlanta,

Georgia, Stuart Deutsch, Georgia Institute of Technology; (2) Charlotte, North Carolina, David Hershel and Ira Hirsch, University of North Carolina; (3) Colorado Springs, Colorado, Major Owenby and Howard Black; (4) Omaha, Nebraska, Frank Dunford, David Huizinga, and Del Elliott, Behavioral Research Institute, University of Colorado, Boulder; (5) Metro-Dade County, Florida, Anthony Pate, Police Foundation, Washington, D.C.; (6) Milwaukee, Wisconsin, Lawrence Sherman, University of Maryland and the Crime Control Institute.

The vehicle for the selection of sites was competitive peer review. The NIJ (1986) issued a formal Request for Proposals (RFP) to elicit proposals for research on domestic violence replication experiments. An ad hoc review group was appointed to examine these proposals and recommend grants for award based on merit. The review panel included academic researchers, police executives, and institutional researchers. NIJ staff had the responsibility of recommending meritorious proposals for funding to the NIJ director, James R. Stewart. The Omaha, Nebraska, replication was submitted prior to the issuance of the RFP. The Crime Control Theory program of NIJ and its peer review panel recommended the Omaha proposal for funding. Five additional police jurisdictions were then selected from about twenty RFP applicants. (Sherman and Berk [1984] and Sherman and Cohn [1989] report on the experiment in Minneapolis; and Dunford, Huizinga, and Elliott [1990] and Dunford [1987] report on the experiment in Omaha.)

Variability Across Sites

The replication program involved six independent experiments at separate sites, each committed (at least) to understanding whether arrest works better than one or more alternative treatments. (The Omaha test was fielded prior to the RFP awards, so PRT did not exercise any oversight over design and initial field implementation in Omaha.) This bald description disguises variability, of course. Variability and mechanisms to accommodate it are important in any multisite collaborative effort.

The NIJ (1986) approach to replication was designed to ensure the independence of investigators at the proposal stage, a guideline compatible with the scientific principle that any given experiment must be independent of another if the results are to be clear and reliable. This principle does not mean, of course, that a given experimenter must avoid learning from others. And to the extent that learning occurs, no experiments are fully independent.

NIJ also recognized but rejected a proposal to have a single investigator mount six independent experiments. (There was, indeed, one such proposal after the Minneapolis experiment, but NIJ decided to fund multiple investigators rather than a single investigator.) This option has advantages over funding individual investigators for multiple sites. For example, it simplifies the grant review and monitoring processes. To facilitate open competition for independent replications, NIJ's request for proposals was general; any police department or research entity that met its requirements for funding was invited to submit a proposal. With the aim of going beyond simple replication of the Minneapolis experiment in order to discriminate among alternative strategies to reduce violence, NIJ staff and management recognized that however praiseworthy the common aim and however virtuous the peer review process, some mechanism had to be developed to identify and bring order out of diversity. Police departments, for example, differ in structure and operating style, as do many community-based organizations. Some are hierarchical and quite centralized, others are less so. Researchers who encourage and collaborate with police departments to do research also differ appreciably in their backgrounds and methods. Some have considerable knowledge of domestic violence or experience in drug field experiments; others have experience as police officers.

Results of the experiments can also be expected to differ from site to site on account of differences among the populations served, ordinances that govern misdemeanor violence cases, the amount and character of domestic violence case flow, the ways that discretion is exercised in the criminal justice system, and so on. This variability, of course, imposes great analytical demands, most notably for consolidation of data to produce a general policy statement that is sensitive to site-based differences.

Program Review Team's Missions and Composition

The Program Review Team (PRT) was created to address the need for oversight and coordination and to better understand the policy and science implications of the SARP experiments. Although the PRT approach is akin to maintaining an active advisory group, it goes well beyond the most active of such groups in important respects. PRT, in the best of cases, delves deeper into independent projects, provides better advice to the sponsors of multisite projects, and produces good science and solid policy advice based on examination of all experiments.

Missions. The PRT had several missions: review the progress of individual experiments, advise NIJ on continued funding for each site, undertake frequent, periodic reanalyses of data produced in the experiments, and conduct cross-site analyses of experimental results.

The first mission, to review progress, is a common one for advisory boards. The PRT deepened this mission in that review is frequent, entailing quarterly meetings of all PIs, PRT members, NIJ program managers and executives, and relevant staff. Relevant staff here included police officers with substantial responsibility in the experiments (see Boruch, Reiss, Larntz, and Garner, in press).

With the second mission, to advise, in mind, at the outset each SARP site was funded on a conditional basis for eighteen to twenty-four months. Continued funding depended on the project meeting its goals for that period and its proposal for completion. The PRT reviewed the progress of each team and advised NIJ on any conditions for continuing funding.

The third mission, to routinely analyze the data generated at each site, served to enhance quality control of data and documentation and to ensure that the disparate projects produced results on a reasonable schedule. This mission exceeded the mandate of a conventional advisory board. It was demanding of PIs, PRT members, and NIJ managers.

The fourth mission, to conduct cross-site analyses, was essential to producing a well-articulated policy statement on the relative effectiveness of various approaches to reducing domestic violence. Reports produced by individual PIs are likely to be locally helpful, but differences in results among sites are likely to confuse a nonscientific audience, including policymakers. At worst, unevaluated differences among sites can undermine the credibility of PIs and the research enterprise.

Composition. The PRT members were selected on the basis of expertise by NIJ. PRT members' expertise covered the major theoretical, methodological, and policy areas in such research. The team included Al Andrews, chief of the Peoria, Illinois, Police Department (police operations), Robert Boruch (research policy and methodology), Lucy Friedman (victim services), Kinley Larntz (statistics), and Albert J. Reiss, Jr. (research policy, methodology, and sociology).

Such wide-ranging expertise is essential. No set of field experiments in domestic violence can be guided well in the absence of expert counsel on major issues in the research, particularly when there are differences among PIs. Nor would many multisite projects be credible to policymakers, notably police executives, or to scientists without such counsel.

The PRT members had considerable experience in field research, and they were judged as experts on the design, implementation, and analysis of domestic violence experiments and on the relevant policy issues. Andrews, for instance, is an experienced police administrator who has contributed to police research, and Friedman, an administrator of a large victim services agency in New York City, has conducted extensive research to formulate victim services policies and practices. The other academic members of the team had extensive experience in research counseling. But even the kind of PRT described here rarely has the time or the expertise to fulfill all of the missions of multisite experiments.

Two kinds of delegation of responsibility are sensible in a PRT. First, the responsibility for conscientious statistical work needs to be devolved to others. Second, the responsibility for auxiliary studies needs to be given to others. In SARP, the devolution was as follows: Sally Freels of the University of Illinois, Chicago, was given substantial responsibility for reanalysis work.

This entailed creating a system for periodic acquisition of files and documentation, and for file review and data analyses. Auxiliary studies of various kinds were undertaken by Michael Dennis, at the Research Triangle Institute, Alex Weiss, at Northwestern University's Traffic Institute, and PRT members. Dennis (1988), for instance, helped to clarify, in general, the relationship between information sought and the frequency and scope of field experiments needed for adequate data collection, as well as the important influences on the success or failure of the research.

Program Review Team's Operations

Most of the PRT's operations were driven by its missions to review field work and to review and analyze statistical data generated in each experiment.

Review Mission. The PRT's reviews of the progress of experiments entailed quarterly meetings, site visits, and the data analyses discussed below. The participants included the police officer and academic collaborators from each site, the PRT members and their support staff, and NIJ managers. The participation of police officers in an oversight role was essential since police officers in the field were responsible for implementing the selection an treatment phases of the experiments. The quarterly meetings placed considerable burden on the review team to reach consensus on issues, especially on those relevant to cross-site comparisons. The meetings were important because of the need to standardize measures for cross-site comparisons, anticipated difficulty of fieldwork in volatile settings, opportunity for mutual education on problems and possible solutions, and policy relevance of the experiments.

Standardization of measures is critical in any cross-site comparison. In SARP, consensus on measures posed the most difficulties among all of the issues presented for group resolution. The volatility of the fieldwork context was clear. For example, during the course of the experiments, one police chief was fired illegally, sued to regain his position, and was reinstated. At another site, an overwhelming need to focus on drug-related crimes nearly swamped the research enterprise. At still another site, the original PI died during the course of the experiment.

Site instability argues for an administrative mechanism that can sustain, over a two- to five-year evaluative effort, collegial interest, support, and understanding. Despite turnover in personnel due to death, transfer, and resignation, and despite scholarly disagreements, NIJ's goals of understanding how to better plan and implement multisite experiments and how to reduce domestic violence remained paramount. PRT was the vehicle for achieving that understanding.

The general format of quarterly SARP meetings involved having the PIs present data from their experiments and discuss methodological problems. Topics considered early in the sequence of meetings were fundamental:

creating randomization systems, standardizing measures, monitoring and ensuring treatment integrity, assessing quality of measurement, and designing follow-up surveys of victims. Meetings that occurred later in the sequence involved more specialized and technically oriented matters, for instance, sophisticated statistical analyses.

The meetings resulted in a temporary "invisible college." That is, practitioners and researchers who would not have otherwise come together were provided the opportunity to learn from one another about phenomena of common interest. The PIs and practitioners routinely shared core information among themselves, with members of PRT, and with the sponsor, NIJ (see Boruch, Reiss, Larntz, and Garner, in press, for details on data sharing).

PRT members also made visits to the sites involved in the experiments. The primary purpose of these visits was to gain familiarity with local conditions, communications, and police department procedures and practices. The visits also provided opportunities to directly observe the conduct of each experiment. The PRT members rode with police officers during peak periods of violence in order to understand police attitudes and their actual handling of cases from the initial call and dispatch to the arrest and report write-up. The site visits helped to uncover problems for which quick remedial action could be taken, such as faulty randomization procedures, as well as less tractable problems, such as misapplication of the treatments and officer resistance to the experiments.

Data Review and Reanalysis Mission. The NIJ's original program announcement did not require that the independent experimenters employ the same computer software or data systems. This requirement would have not been feasible, given a short time frame and limited resources. Similarly, a standard for statistical data analysis was not specified in the program announcement. As a consequence, data analysis at each site could vary considerably. The timing of victim surveys, for instance, could, and initially did, differ. Nor were any special quality-control initiatives demanded in funding the sites.

The task of bringing order to this variability, so as to increase the quality and interpretability of the data product, was a goal of the PRT. Two major routes were pursued to reach this goal: (1) development of broad specifications for core data and core analyses and (2) development of a system for regular production and reanalysis of data produced at each site.

Specification of what core data should be collected at each site, what data items should be standardized across all sites, and what core analyses should be done was undertaken in two stages. The core data specifications were negotiated with all PIs primarily because the PIs were experts in determining what data could be produced locally, and because they differed in their opinions about when and how to get the data, for example, on whether victim surveys, offender surveys, or both should be undertaken. The core analyses specifications also were negotiated, again because of variations in capacity and willingness of the PIs to engage in various kinds of analyses. Standard survival analysis at all sites would have been desirable, for instance, but not all sites had easy access to the necessary technical support.

The construction of principles to guide negotiations among disparate investigators is essential to the success of multisite experiments. Two principles guided negotiations in SARP. The first, enunciated by NIJ through its research program announcement, was to compare the arrest treatment of the Minneapolis experiment with alternative treatments proposed by investigators. The second, enunciated by the PRT and the NIJ program manager, was to improve on the design, measurement, and analysis features of the Minneapolis experiment to whatever extent possible. Both of these principles contributed substantially to the tentative agreements reached among the researchers and police departments on the minimum data to be collected and on how the data were to be analyzed. These agreements constituted the core analysis requirement.

The system that was created for regular reanalyses of data, by site, consisted partly of policy agreements and partly of operational procedures. The agreements covered (1) standardization of core data and core analyses, (2) production of reports and data by each site, notably quarterly and final reports accompanied by the relevant data sets, (3) assurances that the PIs' proprietary interests in first publication of analyses would be met, and (4) organization of reports.

The translation of these agreements into operations and products occurred at the quarterly meetings of SARP. Each PI was asked to present an updated report on his project and an updated data file and documentation for the preceding quarter. Most of the PIs did so on a timely basis. The data were reviewed, reanalyzed, and summarized during the quarter following each meeting by the PRT staff to establish whether the data provided could indeed be used to produce the original analysis and whether the documentation was sufficient. The quarterly reanalyses of site data served as preparations for cross-site analyses.

Analyses of final data across sites was deemed essential to the formulation of useful policies for police handling of domestic violence and for scientific understanding of deterrence. The object was to analyze the data in ways that identified and clarified consistencies and inconsistencies in treatments across sites. An understanding of when and how a particular approach to handling domestic violence is effective or ineffective is important to police and domestic violence policy. Development of a deterrence theory of why, given the cross-site variation, is important to science.

Program Review Team's Reporting Responsibility

The PRT was responsible to NIJ. Consequently, reports were made directly to NIJ in accord with the PRT missions. In particular, site visits were the basis for reports to NIJ on individual site progress. Reviews of proposals for continuing the experiments formed the basis for the PRT recommendations on continuation, change, or termination in the site's approach to experimentation. Reanalyses produced for quarterly meetings were provided to both the PIs and to NIJ to ensure that anomalies were identified and problems resolved. Cross-site analyses were eventually provided directly to NIJ.

Issues

The PRT approach involves issues that are common to any multisite research endeavor. One of these issues is the choice of the number of sites. The number of sites in SARP was not preplanned. (Indeed, the Omaha replication was chosen independently of the others and could not be fully integrated with them.) Rather, a common heuristic decision rule was invoked: Identify the meritorious proposals and fund as many as possible given available resources. As a practical matter, funds were limited so that the choice of more than six to eight field experiments was unlikely. Six were selected under the decision rule. In retrospect, it is reasonable to ask whether six is "appropriate" in any sense. More generally, how can the number of sites in any given experiment be rationalized?

The rationalization depends partly on what analyses will be done and on how confident the investigators would like to be about the results. Consequently, with respect to SARP, one way to frame the matter is to consider the total sample size necessary to detect the effects of the new treatment, that is, arrest. This consideration involves the combination of all sites in a final analysis. A straightforward statistical power analysis reveals the total sample size required. Sites are then added until this total is reached.

The cities involved in SARP were, however, conceived as independent replications. That is, effects were to be analyzed within city sites rather than at the aggregate level. (Only two of the cities eventually conducted the experiment in the entire city. In the other cities, the experiment was conducted in only selected police districts.) Under this replication model each site was required to produce a sample of sufficient size to detect a specified effect at a high level of confidence. But this criterion is insufficient for rationalizing the number of sites, especially if arrest, for example, does not work in each site to reduce assaults.

Let us suppose that in fact arrest will "work" in 75 percent of all cities. We then ask, how many cities in a small sample of cities would have to be tested in order to encounter at least three cities in which the new treatment works? Exploiting the ordinary binomial probability distribution function, where N is number of sites and k is number of sites in which arrest reduces recidivism, we have the following:

$$N = 6, \; p(k = 3, 4, 5, 6) \; = .97$$
$$N = 5, \; p(k = 3, 4, 5) \qquad = .90$$
$$N = 4, \; p(k = 3, 4) \qquad\quad = .74$$
$$N = 3, \; p(k = 3) \qquad\qquad = .42$$

That is, with six cities we are very likely, almost certain, to discover at least three cities in which arrest works, when the true rate is 75 percent. With only three or four cities in a multisite experiment, there is still a remarkable chance, 26 percent or more, that no successes will be discovered despite the fact that arrest works in 75 percent of all cities.

These probabilities would change, of course, with different assumptions about the probability of success in the total population of cities. For instance, if the true success rate across all cities is 50 percent, that is, arrest would work if tried in only half of U.S. cities, the likelihood of finding at least three successes in six sites is 66 percent.

Benefits and Shortcomings

Based on the SARP experience the major benefits of a PRT approach to multisite experiments, relative to a conventional advisory board approach to multisite evaluations, appear to be the following:

First, the strategy facilitates the generation of data of higher quality, the structure, scope, and verifiability of which are better understood. This benefit exists despite considerable variability in operations at the site level.

Second, the mutual education among PIs, program managers, and the review team is substantial. Virtually all of the meetings between these groups generated new insights about both the fast-changing and the chronic problems encountered during the conduct of the experiments. Also, the meetings produced new information that was disseminated rapidly and with considerable opportunity for criticism and questions.

Third, the approach increases the quality of the experiments. The evidence for this contention lies partly in improvements actually made in, for instance, randomization procedures, analysis, and implementation, beyond the plans laid out in original proposals. The PRT leverage for improvements, of course, depends partly on whether and how the funding agency responds to PRT's counsel. Leverage depends also on the voluntary consensus, building procedure of the investigators, PRT experts, and program managers.

Fourth, the approach facilitates data sharing in that the planned and periodic reanalyses result in better documentation of data and a network of potential users. The repeated use of such data to explore new theories and test new hypotheses is sensible in view of the limited resources available for empirical policy experiments.

In sum, the PRT approach provides considerably more information and the promise of a better product to the sponsoring agency, relative to conventional advisory boards, on account of the quarterly reanalysis of data submitted to the team by each PI. It also provides greater management control to the extent that more information and the efforts of a continuously active PRT enhance such control.

The approach involves less centralized control of the experiments by the sponsoring agency than is the practice of some alternative arrangements. In the Rockefeller Foundation's multisite experiments on minority-parent training programs, for instance, one organization (Mathematica Policy Research) was responsible for all of the random assignments, surveys, and so forth at the sites, though not for the program delivery within each site (see Cottingham, this volume). This alternative approach was in accord with the foundation's view that control should be centralized, partly on account of limited local capacity for conducting experiments (Cottingham and Rodriguez, 1987). In SARP, on the other hand, the responsibility for random assignment and so forth devolved to the PI at each site partly because the requisite skills were available at each site and NIJ's institutional policy emphasized the support of independent investigators and independent experiments.

References

Boruch, R., Reiss, A. J., Larntz, K., and Garner, J. "Data Sharing in Criminal Justice Research: The Spouse Assault Replication Program." In J. Sieber (ed.), *Data Sharing.* Newbury Park, Calif.: Sage, in press.

Cottingham, P. H., and Rodriguez, A. "The Experimental Testing of the Minority Female Single Parent Program." *Proceedings of the American Statistical Association: Section on Survey Research Methods.* Washington, D.C.: American Statistical Association, 1987.

Dennis, M. L. "Implementing Randomized Field Experiments: An Analysis of Criminal and Civil Justice Research." Unpublished doctoral dissertation, Psychology Department, Northwestern University, 1988.

Dunford, F. "Random Assignment: Practical Considerations from Field Experiments." In *Proceedings of the American Statistical Association: Section on Survey Research Methods.* Washington, D.C.: American Statistical Association, 1987.

Dunford, F. W., Huizinga, D., and Elliott, D. S. "The Role of Arrest in Domestic Assault: The Omaha Police Experiment." *Criminology,* 1990, *28* (2), 183–206.

National Institute of Justice. *Replicating an Experiment in Specific Deterrence: Alternative Police Responses to Spouse Assault Research Program Solicitation.* Washington, D.C.: U.S. Department of Justice, 1986.

Sherman, L. W., and Berk, R. A. "The Specific Deterrent Effects of Arrest for Domestic Assault." *American Sociological Review,* 1984, *49* (2), 261–272.

Sherman, L. W., and Cohn, E. G. "The Impact of Research on Legal Policy: The Minneapolis Domestic Violence Experiment." *Law and Society Review,* 1989, *23* (1), 117–144.

Albert J. Reiss, Jr., is William Graham Sumner Professor of Sociology at Yale University, New Haven, Connecticut.

Robert Boruch is University Trustee Professor in the Graduate School of Education and professor of statistics at the Wharton School, University of Pennsylvania, Philadelphia.

Multisite evaluations permit testing of contextual effects and allow for positive adaptations to local circumstances. But they can result in a lack of fidelity to the implementation model, a possibility that must be addressed in evaluation design and measurement.

Using Multiple Sites in Mental Health Evaluations: Focus on Program Theory and Implementation Issues

Carol T. Mowbray, Sandra E. Herman

Because the mental health field lacks accepted causal theories and proven interventions, a demonstration project approach using multisite evaluation (MSE) offers many advantages in the development of program initiatives. Multiple sites permit testing of contextual effects and allow opportunities for positive adaptations to local circumstances. However, these same advantages can present major difficulties in ensuring that MSEs meet standards for scientific rigor and have useable results. Often negative outcomes occur along with a post hoc suspicion that failure resulted from lack of fidelity to model implementation. We advocate special emphasis on program theory and implementation evaluation in order to measure and interpret whether the program is working as it should at each site. Unfortunately, the existing literature is more concerned with measurement application of these concepts at the individual subject level than at the program level, which is more appropriate for MSE. In this chapter, a modified research, development, and diffusion approach is presented as a solution.

Multisite Approach to Development and Evaluation

Faced with decreasing resources for public programs and increasing accountability demands, the Michigan Department of Mental Health has made a commitment to utilize a demonstration and evaluation (D&E) approach to the funding of major program initiatives. When new revenues are received from state or federal sources, allocations to local agencies are

NEW DIRECTIONS FOR PROGRAM EVALUATION, no. 50, Summer 1991 © Jossey-Bass Inc., Publishers given to *demonstrate* specific program models, with adequate resources set aside to *evaluate* expected outcomes. Local agency sites are usually selected on a competitive basis, in response to a request for proposals (RFP) issued by the Department of Mental Health. The RFP specifies a program model, problem situation, and/or target population that the interventions to be funded must address. D&E projects usually run for two to four years. At the end of the demonstration period, the local agency understands that if the program has not met expected performance outcomes, it will not be continued. Using this approach, about one-third of funded programs have been cut during or at the end of their demonstration phases. Projects evaluated as successful are incorporated into the base program funding of their catchment area community mental health board. These programs then become models for replications in other local agencies. State funding for replication projects is also categorical, but there is less intensive evaluation and monitoring. This unique approach to program development and system change has been used consistently by our state agency in the area of prevention services, as well as in the development of innovative alternatives to hospitalization for persons with mental illness, and, most recently, in the expenditure of federal block grant funds available under the McKinney Act for persons who are mentally ill and homeless.

Advantages of the Multisite Approach

One major advantage of a multisite approach is its applicability to the development of model programs. Use of this D&E approach has obviously placed us squarely in the arena of MSE methods many times. We feel that MSE offers many advantages in the mental health field. The primary advantage is that this approach to program development is responsive to major deficiencies in mental health treatment: (1) the lack of agreed-upon theory as to causes and amelioration of mental health problems and (2) the limited number of *proven* interventions. Recent reviews of mental health services research have described psychiatric care as lacking in clear diagnostic boundaries and professional consensus about appropriate treatment methods (McGuire, 1989). It has also been noted that "the diverse admixture of professionals and paraprofessionals who administer mental health services participate in a fragmented system with limited commonality in training, philosophy, therapeutic methods, and objectives" (Gottlieb, 1989, p. 225).

In contrast, the RFPs we issue for demonstration project models are based on interventions that have some proven efficacy, albeit with a different service population or in a more limited service context. For example, a 1985 RFP asked local agencies to submit proposals to replicate a psychoeducational services program in Pittsburgh for families of young adults with serious mental illness. Previous research had demonstrated the effectiveness of this intervention in a large urban setting, involving a private hospital

and above-average income families (Anderson, Hogarty, and Reiss, 1980).
We wanted to determine whether this promising approach of providing
support, counseling, and information to families of the seriously mentally
ill would work in publicly funded community programs and state psychiatric hospitals in Michigan, which typically serve low-income groups.

Contextual Effects. A second advantage of multisite D&E studies is
their ability to detect and examine contextual effects. That is, it is known
that the amount and type of mental health problems vary from one geographical area to another (for example, rural versus urban) (Cleary, 1989),
that treatment context (therapists' philosophies or service agency organizational characteristics) can affect treatment outcome, and that treatment
processes may interact with patient characteristics and life situations to
mediate outcomes (Finney and Moos, 1989). Evaluations of interventions
at multiple sites constitute the only way in which these contextual effects
can be assessed *before* programs undergo broader replication and adoption.

Contextual effects may also provide new knowledge about an existing
model. For example, a study, funded by the National Science Foundation,
of two hundred replications of social programs found that local additions
to models (that is, reinvention of the program with new or altered components) tended to enhance effectiveness (Blakely, Mayer, Gottschalk, Schmitt,
Davidson, Roitman, and Emshoff, 1987). Obviously, only when models are
replicated in multiple sites can local revisions be observed and measured.

A four-site evaluation of a support program for families with members
who have developmental disabilities illustrated effects of program context
and revision (Herman, 1983). In this demonstration project, each site was
to implement a program of supports that included respite care, case management, parent training, in-home interventions, and financial assistance
to meet special needs. While all sites did provide these five services, the
contexts of the preexisting service arrays in the agencies and communities
led to the implementation of different models of service delivery. Such
alterations would not have been evident from a single site. The evaluation
identified four distinct models of service delivery based on the emphasis
each agency placed on particular services relative to its preexisting service
array. Contextual effects were also seen in the populations served. Although
all families had children with developmental disabilities, at one site, run by
a state residential center, families were recruited from out-of-home placement waiting lists or state-run out-of-home placements. Whereas at another
site, where placement in a state-run center was not an available option and
the project was run by an agency specializing in child and family services,
the families served had little or no experience with out-of-home placement.

In implementing the concept of family support, each agency also
engaged in revision of case management such that in one model it was a
high-intensity service encompassing traditional case management functions,
in-home interventions with the family, and parent training, whereas in

another model, the case management function was carried out much more informally. Each handled the financial assistance component differently, with one providing a monthly subsidy with no strings and others requiring a statement of need and prior approval for purchase from a special needs fund. None of these variations would have been evident from a single site. All were equally effective in serving the families in their respective service areas.

Difficulties with the Multisite Approach

For all their positive features, MSEs of mental health programs have a number of problems. First, intervention models are rarely well developed, nor are staff trained in similar intervention philosophies. As a result, what should be an MSE of the same intervention likely turn out to be evaluations of different interventions. Second, both the community and mental health organization in which the intervention is located exert strong contextual effects. These contextual effects necessitate adaptations of the model that may result in substantially different programs being implemented in different locations. Both the characteristics of the sites and the ability of on-site staff to implement the program with fidelity to the model are elements of MSEs that must be carefully assessed.

Site Characteristics. Contextual factors are often found to be of greater variety and impact than is anticipated by investigators. In replicating the psychoeducational model previously described, our intent was to determine if the program worked in urban and suburban settings, so we utilized two sites in each category. However, we found that these sites differed on more variables than those that usually covary with urbanity. For example, the implementing agencies differed in program philosophy (medical versus rehabilitation oriented), comprehensiveness of mental health services, and availability of case management services (so that families were not forced to coordinate services and needs of their family members). Further, the communities differed in the availability of affordable housing (affecting whether or not younger adults were able to move out of the family home), community resource levels (so that families could access the generic services described in the educational presentations), and access to transportation (so that families could attend support group meetings). Rather than having two urban and two rural sites, we had four unique communities, and only one that experienced the expected positive program outcomes found in the original Pittsburgh study.

We then had to try and infer post hoc what *may* have been the most significant differentiating characteristics of the one successful suburban replication versus the two urban sites and one suburban site where the intervention failed. While these results produced challenges that we had not anticipated, we were still better off for having done a multisite study.

We at least knew that in *some* public-sector settings the intervention would work, so the approach was not abandoned. Yet, we were also aware that this model should not be implemented statewide but instead should be carefully replicated in a limited number of communities. Successful handling of external contextual effects in the mental health sector may be a long-range endeavor, dependent on more research to identify and explicate the significant contextual effects and on more resources so that larger numbers of sites are studied.

Fidelity to the Model. Contextual effects that are at least *perceived* as amenable to control in MSEs are those that relate to fidelity of program replication (services being provided as intended) and of evaluation design (data being collected reliably and according to schedule). Other authors in this volume have described the methods that they have adopted to overcome these problems. We certainly agree with the need to pay serious attention to and allocate sufficient time and effort for issues of education, training, motivation, and data quality control with program implementors.

Our most recent efforts with the D&E approach involved allocation of state and federal funds for services to individuals who are mentally ill and homeless. Through two years' worth of funding, we were able to establish nontraditional mental health outreach and housing assistance programs in eighteen different mental health catchment areas, through a RFP process. The evaluation designs were established by the state office, with input from the local service providers. The contract negotiated for each project contained an explicit description of the services to be implemented, including objectives, target population, staff composition and activities, and so on. The evaluation requirements were also made part of the contract, describing data collection forms to be used with whom, by whom, and at what intervals, along with requirements for data submissions and analysis and quarterly progress reports. Acting as grants managers, state program specialists with expertise in providing services to individuals who are homeless and mentally ill are required to review quarterly reports, make site visits, and provide hands-on technical assistance to ensure that interventions are being implemented as intended. An evaluation specialist is available to review data submissions and analysis and make site visits to help ensure the quality of the evaluation component. Additionally, staff at all projects must attend quarterly meetings for training, technical assistance, education, and problem-solving opportunities concerning how to meet the needs of and optimally provide services to persons who are homeless and mentally ill. In other D&E project areas, where a site for the model exists in Michigan or nearby, all newly hired staff are required to spend three to five days at this program site as part of their training, with the site visits and program monitoring carried out, under contract, by the staff of the model program.

Quality Control. While we have found that these steps toward correcting the problems of MSEs are useful and necessary for nurturing ownership, assuring fidelity, and addressing quality control issues, we have also discovered that they are not enough! Furthermore, it appears that the respective implementations of the service model and of the evaluation design are highly interrelated in quality. When either demonstration *or* evaluation are working badly, a close examination usually reveals that they are both failing. For example, Mowbray and Freddolino (1986) describe one of a number of Michigan replications of the program in Assertive Community Treatment, from Madison, Wisconsin, a hospital diversion program for persons with serious mental illness. The services involve a very specific team-based, outreach-oriented, intensive case management approach. Interventions are individually tailored and *all* service needs (mental health and otherwise) of the team's clients are met. Continuity of care is assured, through the team, over a long duration and across the various stages of the client's mental illness. Unlike many other mental health treatments, this program has an explicit, codified model that has been well described in research and treatment literature over the past twenty years.

Administrative and program staff at the demonstration site were sent to visit existing successful sites, which were nearby and were provided ongoing technical assistance from the state mental health office. Data collection forms were developed; a local evaluator was hired and trained in their use; reporting formats were provided and reporting requirements were described explicitly in the contract. Despite these careful and well-thought-out strategies, the agency's philosophy and way of doing business overrode all the training, support, and direction provided, even though the staff were newly hired. That is, in its other programs, the agency utilized a traditional, office-based practice approach and was oriented toward serving clients with less serious impairments who had much more limited needs in terms of extent and duration of services. At the end of three months, it was clear that the program was not diverting clients from hospitalization, as required, nor was it outreach-oriented, utilizing a team versus individual approach, or providing continuous and comprehensive services. Data requirements concerning quality and completeness were also far from the mark. The project did not get on track until about twelve months after start-up, when project funding was threatened and the agency administrator was forced to resign. Unfortunately, however, many program fidelity issues are not so blatant and do not emerge until after the evaluation data have been collected and analyzed. When results are produced that are difficult or impossible to interpret, the evaluator then uncovers qualitative information suggesting that there were fidelity problems.

We have had repeated experiences with D&E projects where we suspected post hoc that failure resulted from lack of fidelity to the original model or that mixed results were due to incomplete implementation of all the model's components. This has led us to now place more emphasis on program theory and implementation evaluation in the MSEs of our demonstration projects.

Strategies for Overcoming Limitations of the Multisite Approach

One strategy for overcoming the hazards of MSEs is an additional emphasis on process data so that threats to validity are known and quantified. We recommend a strong emphasis on program implementation measurement to identify contextual effects and to indicate the extent to which the intervention model is replicated as planned. These program implementation measures cannot be generic. They must be developed specifically for the intervention that is being evaluated. That is, mental health evaluations must first identify the critical elements of their intervention model and develop methods of measuring these elements. This measurement will permit the program implementation evaluation to produce information on the fidelity of the replication vis-à-vis the significant components of the original model, as well as on the extent of local adaptation (innovation) that has been added to the replication. In this way, if MSEs produce different results, their interpretation is assisted by data that indicate whether or not the model was replicated and which aspects of fidelity have contributed to the observed outcomes. This strategy requires close attention to program theory, process evaluation, and the level at which data are collected.

Program Theory. Program theory provides the evaluator with a plausible and sensible theoretical model of how the intervention should work, that is, the program philosophy (Chen and Rossi, 1983; Bickman, 1987; McClintock, 1990). By modeling the implementation of the intervention, one can judge the effects of the implementing organization's characteristics on the process, amount, and types of services delivered; the impact of target group participation or coverage on service delivery; the effects of environmental contextual processes on the program's impact, that is, effective implementation; the robustness or sensitivity of the program to the characteristics of the staff who carry out the services; the sufficiency of resources for accomplishing the delivery of services; and the effects of interorganizational transactions on the ability of the implementing organization to deliver the program. Such a theory can enhance the utility of the evaluation. First, it assists policymakers in understanding whether several different operationalizations of a program work similarly and produce similar effects. Second, the use of a theoretical model expands conceptions of problems and solutions in program implementation by providing a description of program components and their relative importance. Third, a program model helps identify variables that can influence the outcomes of the program. Fourth, unintended consequences of how the program is implemented across sites can be detected. Finally, a program model allows the viewpoints of stakeholders, policymakers, advocates, service recipients, and service providers to be presented.

Process Evaluation. Implementation process evaluation moves from the theory or model of program operation to how the program actually operates and is a critical factor in assessing the validity of the intervention. Program implementation is assessed in terms of *extent,* the degree to which the program is delivered as planned, and in terms of *process theory,* which helps explain why the observed extent was achieved (Scheirer, 1987). Both components of implementation evaluation address the internal, statistical conclusion and construct, and the external validity of program evaluations (Palumbo and Oliverio, 1989). Implementation evaluations across multiple sites strengthen the internal validity of evaluations by addressing selection biases and extent of implementation among various segments of the target population, and by identifying the effects of important intervention variables such as organizational characteristics and processes, and workers' backgrounds and activities, which vary across sites. MSEs of implementation process improve the validity of statistical conclusions by ensuring that sufficient variety in the different ways of implementing a program is available to control for type 1 and type 2 errors due to differences in level of treatment, range of dosages, and evenness with which the intervention is applied to the population. Construct validity is strengthened in MSEs through examinations of a number of plausible operationalizations of the program model. Finally, MSEs permit the program model to be generalized across local political environments, governmental structures, cultural traditions, and organizational arrangements. This generalization strengthens the model's external validity and allows program managers to project the extent and process of implementation at new sites.

Program- Versus Client-Level Data. The approaches of program theory and implementation research in evaluation are relatively new. Measurement tools are not readily available; specific methodologies are not prepackaged for easy use. Significant barriers exist to the routine adoption of these approaches: cost, the lack of experience and training of evaluators, the requirement that evaluators be specialists in the program content (treatment) literature as well as in evaluation methods, the extra time and energy required, and the role problems that implementation research presents for evaluators, for example, the job assignment of ensuring that the program's theory is followed and that the implementation is carried out as expected (Bickman, 1989). The use of these methods in MSEs has not been specifically addressed in the evaluation literature. There appears to be significant confusion as to how or whether program theory and implementation measures can be developed and applied at the program level, as opposed to the individual level. Effective use of these approaches in multiple sites obviously requires attention to program-level theory and measurement, not just to the individual client level.

For example, Finney and Moos (1989) advocate the use of a "concept map" that graphically depicts providers' beliefs about how characteristics of the treatment directly affect expected outcomes or operate through specific intervening mechanisms. However, their examples mix client-level characteristics, such as sociodemographics and personality, with program-level features, such as program quality and characteristics of treatment providers or their aggregate activities. Lipsey and Pollard's (1989) formulation is solely at the individual level, with implementation measured according to the amount of exposure to a treatment, the hypothesized chain of internal changes this exposure produces, and how these internal changes then lead to desired outcomes. These types of implementation measurement focus on "dosage" levels or strength of standardized treatments and do not recognize the possibility that entirely different treatments may be delivered, or that the treatment may have multiple dimensions requiring quantifiably different dosages.

In multiple sites, implementation measurement at *only* the individual level may produce data that are confounded with critical characteristics of the model. For example, in a team-based service delivery approach, how does one assess the affect that variability in staff composition has on client outcome? Do teams that have more nurses than social workers produce better results? Measurement of the amount of service an individual client gets from a nurse versus a social worker fails to recognize that in a team approach such determinations should be based on whether a nurse or a social worker more appropriately meets the needs presented by the client (for example, medical or dietary needs pertaining to entitlements and family relations). If nurses versus social workers are randomly assigned, then investigators are violating the principles of the model that they are trying to test by failing to provide an array of services individualized to client needs.

Techniques. Some "how-to" approaches have presented methods for obtaining program-level data for implementation evaluations (for example, King, Morris, and Fitz-Gibbon, 1987). However, these methods also require modification for MSEs and do not emphasize program theory or implementation measurement. That is, the implementation questions presented are often generic. For example, are there written objectives? How much variation in the program has there been over time? Moreover, the questions may also require substantial judgment by the evaluator. For example, if a theory has directed the implementation, what program features does this orientation require the evaluator to examine? Do the materials fit the program's goals and objectives? Do the activities? What constitute important differences in the activities of the comparison versus treatment groups? In order to provide valid answers to such questions, the evaluator would have to be an expert in the content area of the program. Little methodological guidance is provided to the evaluator when content expertise is required, other than to consult experts in the field or to rely on his or her own intuition and experience.

McClintock (1990) has provided the most useful guide yet published on techniques for describing program theory and measure implementation in MSEs. McClintock's approach involves development of a concept map of the program, including its guiding philosophy, service components, and the causal processes by which it is designed to benefit clients—all program level concepts. This information is gained from the literature, key informants, and interviews with the focus groups and individuals involved in the program model. The concept map is then used to guide identification of the domains of program operations that should be studied in order to determine the relationship between program implementation and client outcomes. A major weakness in McClintock's methods, however, concerns the measurement of program operating characteristics, once the significant domains have been identified in the concept map. McClintock basically relies on the opinions of those operating the program to assess the extent to which the key elements from the concept map are in place in the program. In our experience, such judgments from service providers are likely to be affected more by their own diverse training and treatment philosophies than by what their program is actually doing. Thus, the validity of this measurement approach seems questionable. There is also the issue of positive bias due to the program staff's personal and professional investment in the program.

Another theory-based approach to measuring program operations is described by Scott and Sechrest (1989). A group of expert judges was assembled and provided with descriptions of key elements of the interventions and then asked to rate their adequacy. Apparently, this assessment was done on a qualitative basis and no attempt was made to relate these judgments to client outcomes.

A Modified Research, Development, and Diffusion Approach. Clearly, MSEs can benefit from the perspective of concept map and from the information that approaches based on program theory and implementation evaluation provide. The problem, however, is that the extant literature in general does not clearly present methods with sufficient face validity and specificity for collecting this information at the program level. One exception is Mowbray, Davidson, and Bond (1989), who have developed a valid and specific approach to MSEs in mental health, for the Assertive Community Treatment (ACT) program model. The methods are based on the modified research, development, and diffusion model used by Blakely, Mayer, Gottschalk, Schmitt, Davidson, Roitman, and Emshoff (1987) to assess the fidelity of innovations in educational and criminal justice programs. This approach emphasizes the use of rigorous research in the development of programs and acknowledges the active role of local users of innovative programs in maintaining fidelity to the model and yet introducing new elements or variations. The first step in this model, similar to the step presented by McClintock (1990), is to identify the key components of the model. Domains include program philosophy, facilities and equipment, staffing, staff functions, staff linkages, administrative arrangements, client treatment goals, and community and family involvement. These components are identified through reviews of the published literature on the ACT model, and the information is enhanced by interviews with the original developers of the ACT model. Components selected should be observable, discrete, specific to ACT, and exhaustive, Blakely and his colleagues found that most models could be described by twenty to forty components.

Contrary to claims in other research literature, however, the instrument development phase does not stop at this point of component identification. A second phase involves identifying possible variations in the implementation of these components across sites and grouping the variants as either "ideal," "acceptable," or "unacceptable" exemplifications of the components that they represent. In this approach, then, program theory produces specific components that represent fidelity to the model; fidelity is possibly multidimensional; and it is not simply measured by the number of components in place at a program site but can be represented by scores reflecting the extent of variation at each site according to significant program components. For example, for the ACT model component of staff who operate primarily in an outreach modality, two specific measures of fidelity are as follows:

Measure 1. Amount of time spent out of the office
   Ideal: more than four hours per day
   Acceptable: from two to four hours per day
   Unacceptable: less than two hours per day

Measure 2. Extent of facility space available for individual staff offices
   Ideal: staff share office space
   Acceptable: each staff member has a small, individual office
   Unacceptable: each staff member has a large, individual office

Conclusion

Michigan's D&E approach for new service initiatives offers multiple advantages for the development of mental health programs: a field marked by its lack of established therapeutic techniques and the significance of contextual effects in program implementation. MSEs can provide useful information in both of these areas. However, the latter advantage can also be a major weakness of MSEs when contextual and implementation factors are not adequately examined. A "black box" approach to research, where one examines the inputs, outputs, and outcomes but not the implementation process for the intervention, is clearly disadvantageous in MSEs.

Thus, we advocate that evaluators involved in MSEs do more than the usually recommended activities of training, motivating, and providing technical assistance to program implementors. We have found that attention to program theory and implementation measurement are crucial activities in conducting MSEs. Such activities present challenges and costs to evaluators, however. In newly developed fields, there is insufficient differentiation of individual-level versus program-level measurements, the latter being of most concern in MSEs. The modified research, development, and diffusion approach described here may be useful to some evaluators, but others may not find it applicable to their particular intervention models. We hope that, whether positive or negative, experiences with innovative techniques continue to be prominent in the evaluation literature. As evaluators seek to improve their techniques, performance, and knowledge, their struggles and failures may produce greater long-range success than can be achieved through complacent adherence to the tenets of traditional practice and wisdom.

References

Anderson, C. M., Hogarty, G. E., and Reiss, D. J. "Family Treatment of Adult Schizophrenic Patients: A Psycho-Educational Approach." *Schizophrenia Bulletin,* 1980, *6,* 490-505.

Bickman, L. "The Function of Program Theory." In L. Bickman (ed.), *Using Program Theory in Evaluation.* New Directions for Program Evaluation, no. 33. San Francisco: Jossey-Bass, 1987.

Bickman, L. "Barriers to the Use of Program Theory." *Evaluation and Program Planning,* 1989, *12* (4), 387-390.

Blakely, C. H., Mayer, J. P., Gottschalk, R. G., Schmitt, N., Davidson, W. S., Roitman, D. B., and Emshoff, J. G. "The Fidelity-Adaptation Debate: Implications for the Implementation of Public Sector Social Programs." *American Journal of Community Psychology,* 1987, *15,* 253-268.

Chen, H., and Rossi, P. H. "Evaluating with Sense: The Theory-Driven Approach." *Evaluation Review,* 1983, *7* (3), 283-302.

Cleary, P. D. "The Need and Demand for Mental Health Services." In C. A. Taube, D. Mechanic, and A. Hohmann (eds.), *The Future of Mental Health Services Research.* National Institute of Mental Health, Department of Health and Human Services Publication No. (ADM)89-1600. Washington, D.C.: Government Printing Office, 1989.

Finney, J. W., and Moos, R. F. "Theory and Method in Treatment Evaluation." *Evaluation and Program Planning,* 1989, *12* (4), 307-316.

Gottlieb, G. L. "Diversity, Uncertainty, and Variations in Practice: The Behaviors and Clinical Decision Making of Mental Health Care Providers." In C. A. Taube, D. Mechanic, and A. Hohmann (eds.), *The Future of Mental Health Services Research.* National Institute of Mental Health, Department of Health and Human Services Publication No. (ADM)89-1600. Washington, D.C.: Government Printing Office, 1989.

Herman, S. E. *Family Support Services: Report on Meta-Evaluation Study.* Lansing: Michigan Department of Mental Health, 1983.

USING MULTIPLE SITES 57

King, J. A., Morris, L. L., and Fitz-Gibbon, C. T. *How to Assess Program Implementation.* Newbury Park, Calif.: Sage, 1987.
Lipsey, M. W., and Pollard, J. A. "Driving Toward Theory in Program Evaluation: More Models to Choose From." *Evaluation and Program Planning,* 1989, *12* (4), 317–328.
McClintock, C. "Evaluators as Applied Theorists." *Evaluation Practice,* 1990, *11* (1), 1–12.
McGuire, T. G. "Financing and Reimbursement for Mental Health Services." In C. A. Taube, D. Mechanic, and A. Hohmann (eds.), *The Future of Mental Health Services Research.* National Institute of Mental Health, Department of Health and Human Services Publication No. (ADM)89-1600. Washington, D.C.: Government Printing Office, 1989.
Mowbray, C. T., Davidson, W., and Bond, G. *A Multi-State Study of Assertive Treatment Replications.* Lansing: Michigan Department of Mental Health, 1989.
Mowbray, C. T., and Freddolino, P. F. "Consulting to Implement Nontraditional Community Programs for the Long-Term Mentally Disabled." *Administration in Mental Health,* 1986, *14,* 122–134.
Palumbo, D. J., and Oliverio, A. "Implementation Theory and Theory-Driven Approach to Validity." *Evaluation and Program Planning,* 1989, *12* (4), 337–344.
Scheirer, M. A. "Program Theory and Implementation Theory: Implications for Evaluators." In L. Bickman (ed.), *Using Program Theory in Evaluation.* New Directions for Program Evaluation, no. 33. San Francisco: Jossey-Bass, 1987.
Scott, A. G., and Sechrest, L. "Strength of Theory and Theory of Strength." *Evaluation and Program Planning,* 1989, *12* (4), 329–336.

Carol T. Mowbray is associate professor in the School of Social Work and head of the Office of Research at Wayne State University, Detroit, Michigan.

Sandra E. Herman is senior evaluation specialist in the Services Research Division, Bureau of Program Development and Quality Assurance, Michigan Department of Mental Health, Lansing, Michigan.

*Rigorous evaluation of a few, rather than many, sites can uncover
new program strategies.*

Unexpected Lessons: Evaluation of Job-Training Programs for Single Mothers

Phoebe H. Cottingham

Multisite evaluations (MSEs) offer a fast means of learning about a program's universality or replicability. By spreading the evaluation sample over sites, they require less time to build a desired sample. And by showing that a program or treatment works in different local contexts, they speed acceptance or adoption of new program strategies.

MSEs present challenges too. Sites may implement the program differently, or with different degrees of quality. MSEs are not tailored to detect site-specific effects, so evaluators risk ending up with a pooled or multisite data set that leaves questions unanswered.

In this chapter, I describe a multistage MSE that evolved into a multi-treatment evaluation. The evaluation design was restructured after two years of early site learning to capture possible site differences in program implementation. The case in point is the Minority Female Single Parent (MFSP) study, a six-year, $12 million demonstration of job programs for single mothers. The purpose was to test new comprehensive programs created to help low-income single mothers get jobs.

In the first stage, the MSE proceeded on the assumption that all sites would be basically similar in their program content. Thus, a multisite evaluation based on pooled analysis was planned. Early on in our interaction with the sites, we were led to reexamine this assumption of program similarity. Midstream, we redesigned the evaluation to measure effects of the comprehensive programs at four of the six sites.

Without the adaptive, multistage, multisite strategy in MFSP, it is doubtful that the evaluation would have discovered the promising new program model used in one site. The pooled or multisite design originally contemplated did not permit rigorous impact findings by sites.

The restructuring had costs—of more time, funds, and uncertainty. The findings, however, led to isolation of two distinct program models: (1) *schooling first,* followed by job placement or specialized job training, and (2) *training first,* without the academic preparation. The first model, used in three sites, proved ineffective. The second model proved very effective, although it was used by only one site (Burghardt and Gordon, 1990).

The MFSP multisite strategy is traced through four stages in this chapter: (1) initial design and site selection, (2) early learning and a new evaluation design, (3) enrichment of the evaluation, and (4) completion of site operations. A concluding section summarizes the evaluation's key findings and reaffirms the value of site-specific impact studies.

The experience described here may have limited applicability. Complicated social service demonstrations probably warrant this kind of investment and can benefit from flexibility in design strategy. But MSEs that test well-defined, single-treatment variations within known clinical settings might not warrant such high, site-specific investment.

Initial Design and Site Selection

The Minority Female Single Parent (MFSP) program was created in 1981 as a result of a Rockefeller Foundation review of minority-group progress in America. By focusing on a "new problem" facing America—increasing numbers of poor minority households maintained by single mothers and children—it was hoped that other new initiatives or policies might be encouraged at a time when government policy was moving away from poverty programs. Grounded in the assumption that increasing the rate of employment and earnings of single mothers could reduce poverty, the Rockefeller Foundation set two objectives: support direct provision of services to the mothers and obtain new knowledge about what works.

These objectives led to support for nonprofit, nongovernmental organizations as the service providers for single minority mothers (with at least one child under the age of eighteen) who wanted to get a job and become economically self-sufficient. Initially, the plan was that up to six community-based organizations (CBOs) would receive substantial support for up to five years for the services offered to the mothers, services created around the CBOs' perception of mothers' needs and how best to get the mothers into local jobs.

The ultimate objective of MFSP was to provide new knowledge about programs and policies. To achieve this objective, an evaluation of the CBO programs was mandated, to be undertaken by an independent research contractor. The sites, therefore, were not asked to handle both the services and the evaluations; their job was to focus on what they knew how to do—

help poor mothers get ready for and actually take up jobs. This design differs from many MSEs operated from a clinical perspective, since the service provider and the researcher are often the same in each case.

To build a cohesive set of services—from intake, counseling, education and training, support needs, job placement, to follow-up—the sites were assured of up to five years of funding, with annual budgets of $500,000, half provided by the Rockefeller Foundation. Based on prior employment-training experience, these funds permitted enrollment of 200-250 women a year in job preparation services that, on average, lasted for six to twelve months.

Selection of Demonstration Sites. To select sites, organizations needed to have prior employment-training experience and be affiliated with a regional or national employment-training organization (to encourage dissemination and faster replication later). From ten organizations that fit the selection criteria, six sites were chosen to receive grants. The selection took about four months, with request for proposals (RFP), site visits, and reviews by a national advisory panel. At least three national organizations issued their own RFPs among affiliates to nominate site representatives of their respective philosophies and experience to the Rockefeller Foundation.

Even at this early stage, the CBOs differed in program philosophy and operations, despite the specification that seven program components had to be in each CBO plan. All of the CBOs, however, worked toward the same objective: preparing and placing as many single mothers as possible in private-sector jobs.

Multisite Research Design. We asked research contractors to bid on the evaluation and monitoring system, and to propose how they could best use a limited research budget to answer seven research questions. The Rockefeller Foundation oversaw the CBO programs. The research contractor worked with the sites in designing and implementing a management information system, as well as in collecting evaluation data.

The budget of $1.2 million for an evaluation of six sites later proved unrealistic. Another stipulation—that the evaluation would not test or assess particular public policies and would not generate cost-benefit analyses of project performance and participant outcomes—was dropped several years later when a randomized design was introduced. Instead, the research contractors who submitted bids initially were encouraged to propose non-randomized designs, such as comparison groups and synthetic control groups. A five-year time frame was set for the evaluation.

The design chosen called for drawing participant and comparison groups in each site during the first two years, with a twenty-four-month follow-up. The comparison group was drawn from household surveys in comparable neighborhoods but removed from the CBO catchment area. In-person baselines were conducted with both groups, and the site samples were pooled later for impact analysis. Program activity records on each participant were filled out by CBO staff to record services and movement in and out of the program. Another part of the multisite plan was the training of on-site observers or part-time, local researchers to log weekly information, with questions developed by the project manager. These logs were another means of obtaining information on site implementation, as well as of pursuing in-depth study of key issues in program service.

Early Learning and a New Evaluation Design

Much of our early learning was the product of direct contact with the service providers. The management information system took longer to give feedback on how the programs were doing. All program operators expressed alarm about the poor, basic skills of many applicants to their program. Child-care assistance was another focus of site concern. Many of the programs had served women in the past, even single mothers on welfare. But few had deliberately targeted their programs to mothers with preschool children. Employment and training services for welfare mothers in the 1970s typically "exempted" mothers if they had preschool children. And most program operators had previously been encouraged by funders to serve those whom they thought were most likely to move into jobs, which meant people with better education or academic skills. Performance standards also encouraged programs to "cream," that is, to select the most motivated, the most ready. The Rockefeller Foundation, however, encouraged the experimental creation of services for people who faced multiple barriers.

Serving people most disadvantaged in job skills caused problems for the CBOs. Staff members were enthusiastic about the opportunity to work with the target population. But they were perplexed by the poor academic preparation and by the never-ending family pressures and responsibilities that seemed to hinder many program participants. Often these concerns disrupted smooth intake procedures. Mothers would not return, or they would test too low for government-funded training. Delays in processing applicants complicated the enrollment in program services. When programs sought to hold onto new clients, with inadequate or inappropriate services, too much was going on at once. In retrospect, this period of learning, in creating program models, was inevitable and the evaluation phase should have been delayed until the shakedown period was over. (Some evaluators believe, however, that social programs are always in motion, that there is no steady state.)

The implementation issues at the sites brought the evaluation into question. An independent consultant reviewed both the site operations and the evaluation. Rather than urge pullback, the consultant recommended strengthening the evaluation design and concentrating evaluation resources on the most promising sites. Despite the turbulence in the sites, provision of employability services to welfare mothers with very young children was important enough to invest more deeply in the MSE.

Experimental Procedures to Obtain Control Groups. A key change was to drop the quasi-experimental plan—samples of participant and comparison groups in all six sites—for evaluation by experimental methods in sites that agreed to the procedure. The quasi-experimental design failed to control for factors such as motivation. With random assignment of all applicants to either the program or to the control group, the evaluation was able to detect changes in employment and earnings due to the availability of program services. Review of nonexperimental evaluations in the 1970s had brought a new consensus among governmental agencies that experimental methods should be mandated in major evaluations of employment-training services.

Sites Agree to Random Assignment. A special problem was renegotiating agreements with the sites. Since the use of random-assignment procedures during intake was not part of the original agreement, the Rockefeller Foundation offered increased funding to help handle the increased recruitment and intake costs created by our doubling of the number of applicants.

Site staff now had to inform applicants in orientation sessions that they had a 50-50 chance of getting into the program. This advisory presented problems for staff who were, at the same time, trying to encourage people to come into a program and receive help. We found that in all cases, from the head of a CBO to the intake worker, it was important to stress that the program services were available only in the research demonstration, not as a regular program. Special training, site visits, and workshops helped the site staff implement random-assignment procedures.

Sites Dropped from Evaluation. Four of the six sites were asked to participate in the new evaluation. The other two sites were operating at lower levels of enrollment and were judged too weak to warrant the new investment in rigorous evaluation. These sites received diminished support. From the original MSE design, however, one-third of the original sites were dropped from the evaluation.

Site-Specific Samples Replace Multisite Sample. The early learning phase forced acknowledgment that the site differences—both in the program and in the local population served—required expansion of the sample size to capture site-specific impacts. Analysis of baseline and program data from the first year showed site-specific differences in the applicant pool and rate of program entry. Sample targets were reestimated using actual participation rates rather than the rates that the sites projected in their original proposals. The dominant factor, however, was the evidence that each site seemed to have program designs that differed in important ways. Site-specific sample requirements were roughly twice the original numbers for the multisite sample. These new sample targets, when lined up with more realistic projections of site enrollments (based on the first two years of operations), led to a time horizon of two to three years to enroll site samples of one thousand to twelve hundred participants. Instead of five years, six years eventually were needed to conduct site operations, and the evaluation time stretched even longer.

Management of the Multisite Demonstration Strengthened. The Rockefeller Foundation increased its project staff to provide more contact with the sites on operational issues. The evaluation contractor was supervised by a part-time consultant to the foundation, who also interacted with the sites. The budget naturally controlled both site and evaluation activities, with extensive work plans and budgets that required a great deal of monitoring. Although the sites started out with grants from the foundation, performance monitoring forced tighter linkage of the site budget with performance objectives, such as the number of new applicants recruited each month and the number of participants entering education or training classes.

Enrichment of the Evaluation

As we learned from the sites about the difficulties they encountered in trying to help the mothers train for jobs, evaluators feared that the hurdles—especially poor, basic skills—would fail to produce the desired outcome of jobs. Indeed, sites were assigning many applicants to remedial education programs as their test sores for basic skills were too low to meet entry requirements of most job-training programs. Meanwhile, national concern over the increasing numbers of single mothers and children in poverty meant that investments in learning from the sites could have high payoffs.

These two concerns—that real job impacts might be very delayed and that we were in the middle of an important social problem—brought more funds into the evaluation. At the same time, a new research contractor took over the expanded assignment in response to our RFP that set forth the new evaluation objectives.

New Outcomes Measures. Site reports of the barriers mothers faced in successfully completing the program and finding jobs led us to look for short-term measures that could capture the changes in attitudes or behavior in addition to the economic outcomes. By broadening the search for program impact, the aim was to discover noneconomic changes such as parenting attitudes, depression, MSE, and additional schooling or certification.

Cost-Benefit Study. With the deepening of our investment in the MSE, a study of costs and the incorporation of a full cost-benefit analysis added to the scope of the evaluation. Full program costs for the fourth year of operations were obtained, using administrative records and other techniques (Handwerger and Thorton, 1989).

New Follow-Up at Twelve Months. Analysis of the twenty-four-month follow-up survey, conducted in several sites with the quasi-experimental sample data (fielded before this sample frame was dropped in favor of the new experimental sample), revealed a substantial loss of the sample. A twelve-month follow-up sample was instituted in the experimental sample, later a 30-month follow-up survey was conducted.

New Approach for Implementation Studies. Initially, the plan was to use on-site observers as the key sources of information about how the sites carried out their programs. The observers offered fascinating insights into program operations, but this scheme failed to give a cohesive picture across all sites. The on-site researchers were dropped in favor of structured site visits by regular research staff from the evaluation team. This procedure brought greater consistency in what was studied. Later, it facilitated cross-site impact comparisons. Better coverage of operational issues that had generalizability still permitted in-depth consideration of such issues as how women were recruited to the programs, how basic-skills deficiencies were identified and handled, how job training was designed, and how project services were located within the larger organizational structure.

Technical Assistance for Sites on Basic-Skills Strategies. Poor basic skills were a constant complaint in all six sites. A team of literacy specialists visited the sites and conducted workshops to introduce new techniques of instruction, such as newsletters and journals written by the program participants. One site, a large CBO in California with many service centers, immersed their staff in literacy workshops with the literacy specialists.

Special Evaluation of Basic-Skills Strategy. The literacy approach was promising. A special evaluation was designed to see if the immersion of staff in literacy training at the California site made a difference. The evaluator used discontinuous time-series analysis of classroom literacy "events" to measure before-after levels of literacy in classroom activities. Despite turbulence in the site at that time due to external factors, the evaluators detected increased literacy activities in the four training classrooms used for the evaluation.

Child Outcome Measures. A frequent observation from site staff and participants was the positive impact of the training program on mothers' well-being in general, which in turn had positive impact on their children. To capture these two-generation program effects, researchers attempted to add child-outcome measures to the battery of outcome measures in the follow-up instruments.

A major social experiment in the 1970s, the Income Maintenance Experiment, offered persuasive evidence of these program effects, as measured by school records of attendance and test scores (Maynard, 1977; Mallar and Maynard, 1981). The question was how to gain access to individual school records for children whose mothers were in the MFSP evaluation sample. A pilot study estimated the costs of collecting school records. Public school officials in two sites agreed to cooperate but required parental permission. Each parent also had to be contacted through follow-up survey techniques. Even with permission in hand, the records would have had to be collected from the many schools by means of manual collection proce-dures. Faced with high costs of data collection, the child-outcome study was abandoned.

Additional Independent Studies. The richness of the three-year eval-uation in four sites stimulated the funding of new, smaller studies. The site staff were highly cooperative with the additional rounds of visitors, which gave them new opportunities to interpret their program experience.

Two special projects were designed to record how the sites reacted to and accommodated the random-assignment procedures in their outreach and intake processes. A university team of researchers visited the sites and con-ducted a telephone survey with a small sample of women to record their per-ceptions of the "fairness" of randomization (Boruch, Dennis, and Carter-Greer, 1988). Also, a television producer created a video to help funders and other program operators understand why and how random-assignment tech-niques were critical to social program evaluation (Daniel, 1989).

Another university research team used ethnographers in two sites to gain new insights from the mothers about the program and their families in an effort to understand program retention problems. A key conclusion from this work was that the mothers were strongly connected to friends and family members who influenced their participation.

If the family approved of the program goal, getting a job, they were supportive. If they were unhappy about a mother going to work, they could pressure her to drop out.

Management of Site Turbulence. Textbook descriptions of evaluation assume steady-state flows of applicants, retention of staff, and continuity of funding. None of these was true in the MSE for MFSP. The sites experienced year-to-year vicissitudes in grants from governmental funding agencies. Also, there were the usual internal problems of staff turnover and program restructuring.

Nevertheless, by applying Rockefeller Foundation funds flexibly, some of the turbulence was countered. For example, when other funding sources were thin, foundation funds were used to cover more training slots or to pay for more child care. Site visits helped to diagnose and solve problems and to reach agreement on budget line modifications. This flexibility in budget appli-cations was possible because the site operations were supported by the same agency supporting the evaluation. Sites were responsive because of the direct link between the evaluation monitoring and their provision of site services.

Completion of Site Operations

Sites received support as long as they were enrolling the research sample. But the services also needed to be funded after the sample was filled to ensure that those who entered last got the same treatment as the rest of the sample. The key to managing the funds was forecasting when the applicant flow would produce enough to fill the evaluation sample. The slower the intake, the more costly the MSE.

The sites varied in their intake rate. One site looked quite effective (the impact data later confirmed the impression). We decided to invest extra resources to encourage this site to increase its intake. The research contractor developed an innovative strategy that offered incentive payments for new enrollees recruited by the site.

The site in question had been recruiting about twenty-four women a month, but the monthly rate had fallen to eighteen women a month during the third year. The incentive to the site was in the form of premiums for rapidly recruiting the additional numbers over a seven-month period: for each new enrollee brought into job-skill training, the CBO received an extra $1,000, for up to 39 enrollees; $1,500 for the next 20 enrollees; and $2,000 per enrollee thereafter. This system proved very successful, especially during the last months, when 211 women came through random assignment, about 50 women per month. The incentive system resulted in a $78,000 bonus to the site for this extra recruitment.

From In-Depth Studies to the Larger Picture: Unexpected Findings

As the discussion shows, the MSE for MFSP grew in complexity over time. Many facets of site context were studied (Hershey, 1988; Burghardt and Gordon, 1988; Handwerger, Strain, and Thorton, 1989). Most important, an investment in very large samples at each site was made without much certainty that the findings would prove useful to public policy. In theory, three kinds of results were possible: all of the sites had program impacts, none of the sites did, or some did and some did not.

The mixed pattern of results emerged quickly in the analysis of economic impacts at the twelve-month follow-up. In three of the four sites there were no detectable economic effects. At the fourth site the effects were quite remarkable: a 27 percent increase in employment and a 47 percent increase in earnings for mothers who were in the program, compared with the control group of mothers who were not (Gordon and Burghardt, 1989).

To understand these site differences, the researchers examined the implementation studies. After much sifting of evidence, they identified program design as the key explanatory factor. The program design factor revolved around the role of schooling within the program. In the three no-effect sites, great emphasis was placed on basic-skills testing and remediation as a precondition to job training and placement. In the fourth, high-impact site, direct entry into job training was possible for all applicants, with no schooling or test-score requirements.

Without the large samples drawn for each site, the researchers would not have been able to draw such a conclusion. A pooled analysis, combining data from all four sites as if they were the same, would have been misleading (see Figure 1). The strong impact at one site was enough to statistically swamp the no-effects findings at the other three sites, and to produce modest effects overall for the programs. Without the ability to detect site-specific differences, the researchers would have concluded that *all* the programs had a modest impact, when in fact *only one* program had significant effects—very large effects, in fact.

Before releasing the twelve-month findings, however, the researchers examined the alternative hypothesis that effects from the schooling-first programs were simply delayed. Basic education might pay off later. The researchers analyzed thirty-month follow-up interviews for about half the sample (the other half of the sample was still in the field). This analysis showed a continuation of the twelve-month pattern, making it unlikely that the full thirty-month sample would show marked changes.

Coincidentally, a federal law, the Family Support Act of 1988, created a new national program called Job Opportunities and Basic Skills (JOBS) to move low-income mothers from welfare to work. Up to $1 billion a year was targeted for extensive education and employment preparation programs. The MSE for MFSP offered the first rigorous study of education and training strategies now set as a goal for JOBS programs (Hollister, 1989).

The relevance to a major new federal program could not have been predicted at the time of the MSE. Deep investment in the MSE came from our recognition of the centrality of the poverty problem in single-mother families, and from a belief that by keeping a rigorous evaluation going despite the vicissitudes of site operations, something new could be learned.

Implications

For MSEs that encourage local social program experimentation, attention to the possible emergence of strong site differences is essential. It is wise to make these differences explicit and to invest additional resources in studying each site as a treatment. This approach naturally demands flexibility and access to additional resources. Given fixed budgets, there is a trade-off in favor of studying fewer sites, with enough resources to capture site differences, rather than placing total emphasis on testing a single treatment through multisite experiences. The latter may be applicable when site programs are created from a central unit. But when sites are given more autonomy, it is quite likely they will develop different and important strategies that deserve in-depth study.

References

Boruch, R. F., Dennis, M., and Carter-Greer, K. "Lessons from the Rockefeller Foundation's Experiments on the Minority Female Single Parent Program." *Evaluation Review*, 1988, *12* (4), 398–426.

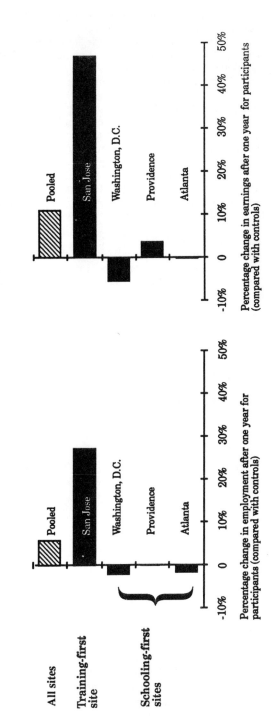

Figure 1. Multisite Evaluation of Job Programs for Single Mothers: Pooled Findings Obscure Important Site-Specific Findings

Employment

Earnings

Note: The effects in three schooling-first sites were inconsequential and not statistically different from zero at the 99 percent level of confidence. The effects in the training-first site are statistically different from zero at the 99 percent level of confidence. The employment effect for the pooled sample is not statistically different from zero, but the pooled earning effect is statistically different from zero at the 90 percent level of confidence.

Source: Gordon and Burghardt, 1989, Tables 2, H-2.

Burghardt, J., and Gordon, A. *The Minority Female Single Parent Demonstration: Local Context and Target Population.* New York: Rockefeller Foundation, 1988.

Burghardt, J., and Gordon, A. *The Minority Female Single Parent Demonstration: More Jobs and Higher Pay: How an Integrated Program Compares with Traditional Programs.* New York: Rockefeller Foundation, 1990.

Daniel, P. *Irrefutable Evidence.* Videotape and brochure. New York: Rockefeller Foundation, 1989.

Gordon, A., and Burghardt, J. *The Minority Female Single Parent Demonstration: Short-Term Economic Impacts.* New York: Rockefeller Foundation, 1989.

Handwerger, S., Strain, M., and Thorton, C. *The Minority Female Single Parent Demonstration: Child Care Referral Options.* New York: Rockefeller Foundation, 1989.

Handwerger, S., and Thorton, C. *The Minority Female Single Parent Demonstration: Program Costs.* New York: Rockefeller Foundation, 1989.

Hershey, A. *The Minority Female Single Parent Demonstration: Program Operations.* New York: Rockefeller Foundation, 1988.

Hollister, R. *The Minority Female Single Parent Demonstration: New Evidence About Effective Training Strategies.* New York: Rockefeller Foundation, 1989.

Mallar, C. D., and Maynard, R. A. "Effects of Income Maintenance on School Performance and Educational Attainment." In A. Kahn and I. Sirageldin (eds.), *Equity, Human Capital, and Development.* Greenwich, Conn.: JAI Press, 1981.

Maynard, R. "Effects of the Rural Income Maintenance Experiment on the School Performance of Children." *American Economic Review,* 1977, 67 (1), 370-375.

Phoebe H. Cottingham is associate director of the Equal Opportunity Program at the Rockefeller Foundation in New York. The Rockefeller Foundation is not responsible for the content of this chapter.

Groups and organizations, like individuals, have "personalities" that can affect program outcomes.

How Organizations Differ: Implications for Multisite Program Evaluation

Stephen J. Guastello, Denise D. Guastello

Modern personality theory seeks to explain individual behavior in terms of interactions between individual differences and environmental variables. Similarly, theories of organizational differences strongly suggest that program outcomes can be seriously influenced by organizational differences. Organizations differ along several dimensions of structure and climate. Multisite evaluations (MSEs) are highly recommended to generalize program outcomes over organizational differences, to generalize conclusions over many possible examples of a hypothetical program, to evaluate the equivalence of control groups, and to detect limits to generalizability or the interaction between organizational characteristics and program features. In this chapter we, first, summarize key features by which organizations differ and then, second, describe some industrial MSEs in which organizational differences have been navigated with mixed success.

Differences in Organizational Structure

An organization's structure is classically described in terms of physicalistic features such as size and patterning of authority and responsibilities. Structure variables sometimes have an impact on work behavior and attitudes within the organization.

Tallness, Centralization, Division of Labor. According to Weber (1947), organizations differ in the dimensions of tallness or flatness (greater or fewer levels of authority), centralization or decentralization of work functions or decision making, division of labor, and size. Researchers have tested the hypotheses that flat is better than tall, and that decentralized is better than centralized, but they have not found any impact of these factors on attitudes, attendance, absenteeism, turnover, or performance (Porter and Lawler, 1965). Division of labor refers to the system by which tasks and responsibilities are divided among employees. Psychologically, some methods for dividing tasks are more motivating to employees than are others (Hackman, 1980). A job is considered motivating to the extent that the employee utilizes a variety of skills, performs relatively whole (rather than fractionalized) work, performs tasks that have a large impact on the work of other people, and receives feedback regarding the success of the work efforts. In general, there is a tendency for labor to be divided more narrowly, suggesting poorer task satisfaction, in large organizations than in smaller organizations.

Size, Subunit Size, Span of Control. Organizational size is typically measured by number of employees, as are sizes of work groups and subunits. Span of control refers to the number of people or range of activities under the auspices of one supervisor. At the lowest level of the organizational hierarchy, subunit size and span of control are often the same in scope. In U.S. organizations subunit size appears to be proportional to organizational size, while in Japanese organizations subunit size is more closely linked to technological requirements to operate the organization's technology (Marsh and Mannari, 1981).

Research has shown that increased size is associated with decreased job satisfaction, increased absenteeism, increased turnover (Porter and Lawler, 1965), and increased labor grievances (Churnside and Creigh, 1981; Porter and Lawler, 1965). Argyle, Gardner, and Cioffi (1958) reported a curvilinear relationship between absences and unit size indicating that absenteeism was highest in factor units of twenty to thirty persons, compared to larger or smaller units.

Studies relating subunit size to productivity and accident criteria report a mixture of negative, positive, curvilinear, and null relationships (Porter and Lawler, 1965; Guastello and Guastello, 1987a). Several explanations have been offered to account for these research findings. Large groups tend to be less cohesive, more alienating, and more heterogeneous than is the case with smaller groups. If cohesiveness is coupled with high-performance norms, relatively higher levels of performance would generally ensue (Griffin, 1982). Small groups are too closely supervised in some organizations, thereby stifling individual initiative and autonomy (Ouchi and Dowling, 1977). Therefore, optimal group size within each organizational context balances the autonomy of large groups with the cohesiveness of small groups. Blau (1981) and S. Guastello (1988) observed that size, and perhaps other structural aspects, predisposes organizations to a wide range of changes in behavior. Whether any dramatic events actually occur depends on other matters.

Technology. Woodward (1965) studied the relationship between technology and organizational structure. She identified three configurations:

long-linked technologies, which are characteristic of assembly-line processes; batch technologies, where a variety of tasks can be assigned to the same operators and equipment while preserving the same overall organizational structure; and single-batch technologies, in which products are produced only one or two at a time, and few are ever alike (for example, spacecraft, satellites, research reports).

Single-batch technologies typically involve more innovation per product than is required with the other two configurations. And their organizational structures are often composed of ever-changing task forces rather than of fixed groups. Hence the distinction between organic and mechanistic structure can be made (Burns and Stalker, 1961).

Differences in Organizational Climate

An organization's climate is characterized in terms of the dynamics taking place among individuals and between the individual and the organization as a whole. In recent years the climate concept has evoked into a notion of an organizational culture.

Group Personality. As a pioneer in the study of group and organizational differences, Mead (1934) focused on the concept of group personality. When individuals assemble into groups, the groups take on personalities that distinguish them from other groups, in much the same way that an individual's personality distinguishes him or her from other individuals. The group personality is a composite of individual traits, but the traits held most in common among group members become dominant features of the group personality. Furthermore, the leader's traits receive the most weight in the group personality composite.

In later work, the concept of group personality evolved into the notion of organizational climate and culture, as defined in the theories outlined below. The group remains the basic building block for understanding and changing organizational behavior (French and Bell, 1990). But, as additional analysis has revealed, there appears to be as much variability in climate within organizations as there is between organizations; much of this variability can be traced to the psychological contributions of the organization's top-ranking people (Drexler, 1977).

Humanistic Approaches. Meltzer (1942) offered the first major distinction between organizations by fusing contemporary politics with clinical psychology. A humanistic organization responds to human emotional needs and advocates democratic internal processes. An inhuman organization views its members as machines and adopts policies of exploitation and autocratic, if not fascistic, rule. Meltzer's field research indicated that the functionality of an organization can be improved by humanizing the interpersonal relations of key personnel. His humanistic concept and approach have undergone many embellishments by later theorists.

According to McGregor (1960), behavior in organizations is the embodiment of a set of beliefs about human nature. Organizations operating with theory-X beliefs develop policies under the assumption that the individual has an inherent dislike for work, will avoid work or responsibility, is primarily seeking money and security, and is best motivated to work through coercion and punishment. Theory-Y beliefs hold that work is as natural as play or rest, that people will seek responsibility and exercise self-direction and self-control in pursuit of organizational objectives, and that the ability to exercise imagination and creativity is widespread in the population and generally underutilized by organizations. Based on this contrast, McGregor views organizations that operate under theory-Y principles as more effective than theory-X organizations.

Likert (1961) conceptualized four types of organizations: exploitive authoritarian (system 1), benevolent authoritarian (system 2), consultative (system 3), and participative (system 4). System 1 organizations are closely akin to theory-X organizations. System 2 organizations are no more democratic than are system 1, but rather than exploiting the personnel, the emphasis is on "helping" or "taking care of the employee." In system 3, input from employees is sought on many decisions, and many management-employee discussions take place. Nonetheless, the rank-and-file employees have no consistent opportunities to influence decisions, and their recommendations may or may not be followed. In system 4, employees are actively involved in making decisions. Likert elaborated on how to set the stage for effective participative management.

Traits. Organizational climate research conducted during the 1960s and 1970s focused on empirically derived traits and types. The most common trait constructs found were individual autonomy, rigid versus flexible division of labor, reward and achievement orientation, warmth and support, progressiveness or concern about development, degree of risk taking, and tight versus loose control (or supervision) of activities (Saal and Knight, 1988). Research on organizational climate has also been directed toward specific definitions of climate, such as climate for innovation (Siegel and Kaemmerer, 1978), motivation (Litwin and Stringer, 1968; Maehr and Braskamp, 1986) and safety (Brown and Holmes, 1986; Guastello and Guastello, 1987b; S. Guastello, 1989; Zohar, 1980).

Pathologies. Kets de Vries and Miller (1986) identified five types of organizational pathology, based on commonly recognized clinical classifications: dramatic, schizoid, compulsive, depressed, and paranoid. Dramatic organizations are characterized by excessive risk taking and flamboyance. While assumption of risk often pays off, the organization is often unwise in its choices of risky ventures. Schizoid organizations have difficulty focusing on a business plan, resulting in senseless changes of policy that only serve to confuse the work force. Compulsive organizations place a greater priority on bureaucratic procedures than they do on actually accomplishing needed tasks. Depressed organizations are characterized by poor morale and general lack of energy among employees. Paranoid organizations operate under the belief that entities within and outside the organizations are out to destroy them; work life is riddled with politics and secrecy. In all five pathologies, the symptoms are indexes of critical losses in efficiency.

Culture. The concept of culture entered the literature on organizational differences in two ways. The first invokes conventional notions of culture and nationality, and is typified by theory Z (Ouchi, 1980), which compared American and Japanese organizations. Life in American organizations is typically characterized by individual rewards, tasks defined for individuals, concern with individual career advancement, concern with developing career specialization, rapid advancement within the company, frequent performance appraisals, and centralized control of decisions by management. Japanese organizations, by contrast, are characterized by group rewards, tasks designed for group efforts, concern with long-term commitment to the company, concern with the company as the focal point of one's career development, slow advancement through the corporate ranks, and infrequent individual reviews. Furthermore, in Japanese organizations, the largest possible decisions are pushed downward to the lowest possible person in the organizational hierarchy.

Ouchi (1980) traced differences in social and reinforcement structures to the preindustrial ecologies of Japanese and American farmers. The Americans who grew wheat in the vast flatlands of Kansas required individuality and self-reliance in order to survive. The Japanese who grew rice on paddies in mountainous terrain survived through team work and cooperation.

In its second application, the culture concept is used to describe organizational differences within a society. Lundberg (1985) found several available definitions of organizational culture. Some are more corporate centered, such as "the way we do things around here," or "a general constellation of beliefs, mores, values systems, behavioral norms and ways of doing business that are unique to each corporation" (pp. 170–171). Other definitions are anthropological, such as "the transmitted and created content and patterns of values, ideas, and other symbolic-meaningful systems as factors in shaping human behavior" (p. 170). Organizational cultures can be distinguished on the basis of their artifacts and legends, values and assumptions, climate, and structure.

Van Maanen and Barley (1985) noted that organizational cultures can contain subcultures. Subcultures are often defined in terms of job assignment, status, or equity. Because of the greater homogeneity of members at the top levels of organizations, descriptions of an organization's culture may not necessarily apply to the workers at lower echelons.

Program Evaluations in Work Organizations

Programs most frequently encountered in industry can be placed in one of three categories for our purposes: (1) those that affect individual functioning, such as technical skills or social skills programs, (2) those that affect group functioning, such as team building, conflict resolution, or the installation of autonomous work groups, and (3) those that are primarily directed at the functioning of the total organization, such as restructuring or cultural change projects and a wide class of organizational development (OD) programs. These categories are not mutually exclusive, but they do represent qualitative differences in focus. A successful individual-level program can be expected to have some impact on group- and organizational-level criteria of success. An organizational change project can be expected to have an impact on group and individual measures of performance as well.

Although MSEs in industry are rare, we did identify four topics to which MSEs have been applied. The following examples offer a view of the relative frequency with which MSEs are used, the relative use of survey versus experimental or quasi-experimental evaluations, the use of surveys to customize a program for a site, and the ambiguous role of organizational differences in program outcomes.

Management by Objectives (MBO). MBO is a system of group-oriented goal setting, action planning, and performance appraisal. Kondrasuk (1981) reviewed seventy-six research reports that encompassed 185 evaluated applications of a MBO program. Of the seventy-six reports, thirty-nine were case reports, ten were survey evaluations, twenty-six used quasi-experimental research designs, and five were considered true experiments. Approximately 5 percent of the reports gave specific program descriptions that were sufficient to classify the program as a true example of MBO, 7 percent gave program descriptions sufficient to classify the program as other than a true example of MBO, while the others gave insufficient program descriptions. Kondrasuk observed that there were perhaps as many variations of the program as there were implementations of the program.

Eight out of thirty-nine case reports (fifty-eight applications) were MSEs. Two MSEs used both subjective and objective criteria, while the remaining six did not use objective criteria. Nine out of ten survey evaluations were MSEs that sampled employees from three to nine hundred companies. Of the twenty-six quasi-experimental studies, two could be clearly identified as MSEs; nine used objective criteria, while seventeen, including the two MSEs, did not. Of the five truly experimental evaluations of the MBO, only one was an MSE; it involved thirty-two bank branches and used objective data.

Kondrasuk (1981) concluded that favorable results were inversely related to the rigor of the research design. Quasi-experimental and experimental research designs produced less favorable conclusions than did case studies or survey evaluations. Our inspection of his results revealed that the multisite character of the research design did not favorably or unfavorably affect the evaluation outcome or rigor of evaluation. MSEs appeared to be used mostly to ensure generalizability of the results, rather than to associate program effectiveness with organizational differences. Kondrasuk observed, however, that "there are also tendencies for MBO to be more effective in the short term (less than two years), in the private sector, and in organizations removed from direct contact with the customer. . . . We need more well-controlled [longitudinal] experiments. . . . The control group should be explicitly described. . . . We still need to determine what aspects of MBO are most effective in which situations" (1981, pp. 425-426).

Team Development and Other OD Techniques. Woodman and Sherwood (1980) reviewed twenty-four studies in which the effectiveness of four subvarieties of a team development program were evaluated. Two of the team development studies were MSEs. Overall, the favorableness of the program outcomes was inversely related to the rigor of the program evaluations. Terpstra (1981) reached a similar conclusion regarding a wide range of OD interventions.

Bowers (1973) described a large-scale project in which the effectiveness of five OD techniques was evaluated relative to no-treatment controls: laboratory training (a broad category including, but not limited to, team building), interpersonal process consultation, task process consultation, survey feedback, and data handback. In a survey feedback procedure, the consulting team collects survey data and formally presents the results to all members of the organization through a series of structured meetings. In a data handback procedure, the consulting team imparts the results of a survey to contact persons in the organization, and no provisions are made for comprehensive feedback to organizational members. Participants were employees of twenty-three sites from ten organizations. Program evaluations were based on responses to the Survey of Organizations, completed before and after the intervention. OD techniques were chosen on the basis of the preferences of the organizations' consultants, not on the basis of the initial survey results. Laboratory training resulted in improvements on one of sixteen survey criteria, with declines on two others. Interpersonal process consultation resulted in improvements on seven criteria. Task process consultation resulted in declines on most criteria. Survey feedback resulted in improvements on eleven criteria, while data handback was generally associated with negative change.

We observed that the multisite character of the study provided a variety of OD techniques for study; but since there was no equating of organizations on structural or climate conditions, there was no way to assess the generalizability of the program outcomes over organizational differences. Furthermore, there was no assurance that all examples of the same class of program were really similar.

One of the MSEs reviewed by Woodman and Sherwood (1980) actually pertained to the role of interpersonal trust in the success of OD projects (Kegan and Rubinstein, 1973). Hypotheses concerning the central role of trust could be derived from many of the organizational theories described earlier in this chapter. Three organizations participated in the study; a research and development firm, a chemical manufacturer, and an aerospace manufacturer contributed three hundred employees each. Trust variables were measured by a survey administered before and after the intervention. A potpourri of interventions was involved. Results supported the hypotheses that trust facilitates OD interventions, and that good OD interventions build trust.

Unlike the other program evaluations considered earlier in this chapter, the results concerning trust were generalized over programs. The generalizability over other types of organizational differences was questionable, since no further statistical associations between program characteristics and organizational differences were reported.

Accident Reduction. Guastello and Guastello (1987a, 1987b) developed the Occupational Hazards Survey for diagnosing, explaining, and controlling occupational accident risks. As part of the data feedback strategy, survey results are used to formulate a list of recommended actions specific to the host organization. Ideally, the organization implements the recommendations, either with or without further input from the consultants. S. Guastello (1989) reported on an evaluation of the accident reduction strategies recommended to eight organizations in the secondary metal manufacturing industry. Organizational sizes ranged from 35 to 125 persons. Eight separate intervention programs were issued, which contained ten recommendations in common. Organizations also varied in the degree to which they used formal or informal meetings and memos to convey survey information. Implementations of recommendations were largely confined to the least expensive options.

Effectiveness was measured on the basis of Occupational Safety and Health Administration accident rates before and after intervention. While all eight participating organizations received the treatment, they varied in the amount of time allotted to work with their recommendations before the posttest measures were taken. Both pretest and posttest measures were based on one year of exposure. Results showed that reductions in group accident rates were related to the number of months each organization had to work on its recommendations before posttesting. On average, group accident rates were reduced by 30 percent within a six-month period. Other trends in program success were explicable in terms of initial measurements of safety climate constructs.

Computers and Women. Gutek and Bikson (1985) evaluated the impact of office computerization on the work conditions of women. The job discrimination question is considered secondary in this context because the computer systems were installed to enhance performance and not to specifically affect equality issues. Note that the criterion used was not the effectiveness of the computer system relative to the performance of office tasks but rather the presence versus absence of a secondary impact on job discrimination against women. The sample contained 530 men and women drawn from fifty-five offices in twenty-six private organizations in the Los Angeles area and captured a representative range of professional and clerical jobs.

Gutek and Bikson drew clear conclusions. When educational level was controlled, high-status jobs were occupied by a disproportionate number of men. The computer technology only served to reinforce the subservient role of women in the organizations. Women entered data for use by others. Men accessed the data to formulate ideas and facilitate the performance of other tasks, and they had more opportunities to provide input on the choice of computer systems for the organization. No links to organizational characteristics were reported.

Summary

Our inspection of several MSEs revealed that the prime emphasis of these studies was on extension of generalizability across organizations. Program variability has been treated most often as a nuisance effect, although it was planned in one instance (accident reduction) and managed in another (trust and OD). Control group equivalence was rarely expressed in terms of climate or structure in quasi-experimental or experimental designs. Technology was the most often-noted difference among organizations participating in an MSE. Survey evaluations were more common than quasi-experiments and were occasionally supplemented with objective criteria. In one case survey, data were used to define, rather than to evaluate, the program (accident reduction). It was apparent in two studies (accident reduction, trust and OD) that initial climate conditions affected program outcomes. Overall, the entire matter of the impact of organizational characteristics on program outcomes is underresearched.

References

Argyle, M., Gardner, G., and Cioffi, I. "Supervisory Methods Related to Productivity, Absenteeism, and Labor Turnover." *Human Relations*, 1958, *11*, 23–40.

Blau, J. R. *Organizational Failure: A Longitudinal Study of Architectural Firms.* Conference Report No. 3148. Washington, D.C.: American Sociological Association, 1981.

Bowers, D. G. "OD Techniques and Their Results in 23 Organizations: The Michigan ICL Study." *Journal of Applied Behavioral Science*, 1973, *9*, 21–43.

Brown, R. L., and Holmes, H. "The Use of a Factor-Analytic Procedure for Assessing the Validity of an Employee Safety Climate Model." *Accident Analysis and Prevention*, 1986, *18*, 455–470.

Burns, T., and Stalker, G. M. *The Management of Innovation*. London: Tavistock, 1961.

Churnside, R. J., and Creigh, S. W. "Strike Activity and Plant Size: A Note." *Journal of the Royal Statistical Society*, 1981, *114*, 104-111.

Drexler, J. A. "Organizational Climate: Its Homogeneity Within Organizations." *Journal of Applied Psychology*, 1977, *62*, 38-42.

French, W. L., and Bell, C. H., Jr. *Organization Development: Behavioral Science Interventions for Organization Improvement*. (4th ed.) Englewood Cliffs, N.J.: Prentice-Hall, 1990.

Griffin, R. W. *Task Design: An Integrative Approach*. Glenview, Ill.: Scott, Foresman, 1982.

Guastello, D. D., and Guastello, S. J. "The Relationship Between Work Group Size and Occupational Accidents." *Journal of Occupational Accidents*, 1987a, *9*, 1-9.

Guastello, D. D., and Guastello, S. J. "A Climate for Safety in Hazardous Environments: A Psychosocial Approach." *Social and Behavioral Sciences Documents*, 1987b, *17* (report no. 2839), 67.

Guastello, S. J. "Catastrophe Modeling of the Accident Process: Organizational Subunit Size." *Psychological Bulletin*, 1988, *103*, 246-255.

Guastello, S. J. "Catastrophe Modeling of the Accident Process: Evaluation of an Accident Reduction Program Using the Occupational Hazards Survey." *Accident Analysis and Prevention*, 1989, *21*, 61-77.

Gutek, B. A., and Bikson, T. K. "Differential Experiences of Men and Women in Computerized Offices." *Sex Roles*, 1985, *13*, 123-136.

Hackman, J. R. "Work Redesign and Motivation." *Professional Psychology*, 1980, *11*, 445-455.

Kegan, D. L., and Rubinstein, A. H. "Trust, Effectiveness, and Organizational Development: A Field Study." *Journal of Applied Behavioral Science*, 1973, *9*, 498-513.

Kets de Vries, M. R., and Miller, D. "Personality, Culture, and Organization." *Academy of Management Review*, 1986, *11*, 266-279.

Kondrasuk, J. N. "Studies in MBO Effectiveness." *Academy of Management Review*, 1981, *6*, 419-430.

Likert, R. *New Patterns of Management*. New York: McGraw-Hill, 1961.

Litwin, G. H., and Stringer, R. A. *Motivation and Organizational Climate*. Cambridge, Mass.: Harvard Business School, 1968.

Lundberg, C. C. "On the Feasibility of Cultural Intervention in Organizations." In P. J. Frost, L. F. Moore, M. R. Louis, C. C. Lundberg, and J. Martin (eds.), *Organizational Culture*. Newbury Park, Calif.: Sage, 1985.

McGregor, D. M. *The Human Size of Enterprise*. New York: McGraw-Hill, 1960.

Maehr, M. L., and Braskamp, L. A. *The Motivation Factor*. Lexington, Mass.: Lexington/Heath, 1986.

Marsh, R., and Mannari, H. "Technology and Size as Determinants of the Organizational Structure of Japanese Factories." *Administrative Science Quarterly*, 1981, *26*, 33-57.

Mead, G. H. *Mind, Self, and Society*. Chicago: University of Chicago Press, 1934.

Meltzer, H. "Explorations in Humanizing Relations of Key People in Industry." *American Journal of Orthopsychiatry*, 1942, *12*, 517-528.

Ouchi, W. G. *Theory Z: How American Business Can Meet the Japanese Challenge*. Reading, Mass.: Addison-Wesley, 1980.

Ouchi, W. G., and Dowling, J. B. "Defining the Span of Control." *Administrative Science Quarterly*, 1977, *22*, 357-365.

Porter, L. W., and Lawler, E. E., III. "Properties of Organizational Structure Related to Job Attitudes and Behavior." *Psychological Bulletin*, 1965, *64*, 23-51.

Saal, F. E., and Knight, P. A. *Industrial/Organizational Psychology: Science and Practice.* Belmont, Calif.: Wadsworth, 1988.

Siegel, S. M., and Kaemmerer, W. G. "Measuring the Perceived Support for Innovation in Organizations." *Journal of Applied Psychology,* 1978, *63,* 553-562.

Terpstra, D. E. "Relationship Between Methodological Rigor and Reported Outcomes in Organizational Development Evaluation Research." *Journal of Applied Psychology,* 1981, *66,* 541-543.

Van Maanen, J., and Barley, S. R. "Cultural Organization: Fragments of a Theory." In P. J. Frost, L. F. Moore, M. R. Louis, C. C. Lundberg, and J. Martin (eds.), *Organizational Culture.* Newbury Park, Calif.: Sage, 1985.

Weber, M. *Theory of Economic and Social Organization.* New York: Oxford University Press, 1947.

Woodman, R. W., and Sherwood, J. J. "The Role of Team Development in Organizational Effectiveness: A Critical Review." *Psychological Bulletin,* 1980, *88,* 166-186.

Woodward, J. *Industrial Organization: Theory and Practice.* London: Oxford University Press, 1965.

Zohar, D. "Safety Climate in Industrial Organizations: Theoretical and Applied Implications." *Journal of Applied Psychology,* 1980, *65,* 96-102.

Stephen J. Guastello is associate professor of Industrial-Organizational Psychology and Human Factors Engineering at Marquette University, Milwaukee, Wisconsin.

Denise D. Guastello is assistant professor of psychology at Carroll College, Waukesha, Wisconsin.

The obstacles that hamper multisite evaluations in criminal justice
settings can be overcome through an understanding of how the
criminal justice system is organized and how it operates.

Multisite Evaluations in Criminal Justice Settings: Structural Obstacles to Success

Wesley G. Skogan, Arthur J. Lurigio

This chapter examines some structural impediments to multisite evaluations (MSEs) in the criminal justice domain. Besides the usual methodological considerations involved in conducting credible evaluations, these structural features impose social, political, and organizational constraints on evaluation research, which make MSEs difficult and risky. In this chapter we describe the obstacles to MSEs and then review two projects that succeeded despite these impediments. A third, notable criminal justice MSE, the Spouse-Assault Replication Program, is described by Reiss and Boruch (this volume). These cases illustrate how evaluators might overcome—or learn to live with—the roadblocks to MSEs within the criminal justice system.

There are several characteristics of the criminal justice system that hamper the implementation and evaluation of multisite programs. To begin, the system is extremely *decentralized*. Police departments, for example, can operate within the province of municipalities, counties, campuses, public housing, mass transit, and the states. There are nearly 23,000 independent policing agencies within the United States. The criminal justice system is also highly *fragmented*. Cities administer police departments and jails; counties administer sheriffs' and prosecutors' offices, jails, and probation agencies; state governments run the prisons. Agencies are embedded in disparate political settings, each with its own priorities for taxing and spending. The federal government plays a minor role in financing local systems (only 8 percent of the criminal justice system budget is federal) and in establishing standards and sparking innovation.

Criminal justice agencies are traditionally very *insular*. Limited mobility or interchange occurs across jurisdictional boundaries. This is coupled with a strong sense that local situations are unique and a "not invented here" attitude toward innovation, which is especially prevalent in policing. Many practitioners are not very sophisticated with respect to research; only a high school diploma is required for entry-level positions, and in most places a university degree has not been seen as a prerequisite for promotion into the ranks of management. The research and planning divisions of criminal justice operating agencies typically perform little of either activity; usually their primary task is to draft new forms and internal regulations, and their objectives are narrowly focused. Successes and (especially) failures are not shared among agencies, and information regarding new developments seldom moves beyond department perimeters. In the absence of a tradition of research or even professional communication, no real mechanism exists for broadly communicating about programs or policies.

Because much of their work is *labor intensive*, criminal justice agencies have not faced the prod of technological change. For example, few changes have appeared in the technology of police work since the introduction of car radios in the 1930s, and, if anything, prisons have regressed, becoming more overcrowded and less able to provide services to inmates. The prominent exception to this rule has been the recent development of computer and telephone automation supporting more effective systems of home detention (for example, see Lily, Ball, and Wright, 1987).

Criminal justice agencies also have great difficulty in devising *meaningful performance measures*. This has impeded any substantive focus on enhancement of productivity, a source of innovation in many organizations; criminal justice agencies generate many activity counts but do not have a good handle on their effectiveness at solving their target problems. The lack of standardized performance criteria has made it very easy to manipulate indicators of agency effectiveness; statistics such as a prosecutor's "conviction rate" cannot wisely be taken at face value. Some indices, such as revocation rates in probation, can be double-edged. Violations may be interpreted either as successes (probation officers are agents of the court and their job is to monitor infractions and report them summarily) or as failures (officers are also agents of change and their job is to help offenders relinquish criminal activity).

Criminal justice agencies also foster a *subculture of secrecy* concerning their work. This has several functions: It obfuscates the tremendous discretion that many functionaries in the system enjoy, it shields the general public from the role that violence plays in their daily work, and it masks from view the corruption problems that plague law enforcement. This subculture has serious consequences for evaluators, who are seen readily as "snoops" for management, the courts, or individuals with political agendas. Line staff easily adopt an "us against them" mentality toward outside evaluators. Furthermore, police and correctional administrators work in a heavily unionized environment that sometimes interferes with efforts to redeploy personnel, their only flexible resource.

Criminal justice agencies generally exist in highly charged *political environments*. They are the most visible components of local government, as well as the most expensive, and their actions are frequently monitored by the media, who historically have assumed a watchdog or adversarial posture toward the system (Lavrakas, Rosenbaum, and Lurigio, 1990). Evaluators may document poor or inadequate performance; worse, they may stumble upon evidence of impropriety or malfeasance. Judges, prosecutors, and sheriffs generally are elected officials, and police chiefs and state corrections administrators stand close to their mayors and governors and have a vested interest in seeing them remain in office. Criminal justice policy-making is both emotionally laden and costly, leading everyone involved to try to look good, err on the side of caution, and when in doubt take the conservative course. Researchers easily can seem unappreciative of the sensitive and precarious political environments in which criminal justice agencies exist (Lurigio and Skogan, 1990). Indeed, evaluators would be wise to work in communities with stable political and agency leadership, for a turnover at the top can easily bring in new leaders who are not interested in the prior administration's pet projects.

Finally, the criminal justice system operates within a *context of individual rights*. The participants have a strong sense of legal constraint in procedural issues, an unwillingness to risk injustice in individual cases, and a stated (although not actually delivered) commitment to providing individualized treatment. This translates, for example, into a general aversion to the concept of random or unbiased assignment, which is the hallmark of the best designs for yielding interpretable information about programs.

Two Examples of Multisite Evaluations

These impediments to evaluation in the criminal justice arena can be seen in two multisite programs. The first was an evaluation of new policing programs, which was conducted in multiple neighborhoods in two cities. The second was an evaluation of intensive probation supervision that was conducted in eleven sites across the country. Both the programs and their evaluations were shaped in important ways by the decentralized, fragmented, insular, politicized character of the system in which they were embedded, and by its rights-oriented environment.

The policing evaluation illustrates how innovative program ideas flowed from jurisdiction to jurisdiction, the process by which the original program construct was transformed by local politics and leadership factors, why the agencies wanted to be involved in the MSEs, especially in the development of performance measures, and the politics of disseminating research findings. The probation evaluation illustrates how programs diverged from place to place, how the discretionary nature of the probation process shaped everything from the client pool for the evaluation to the out-

comes measures, and the problems involved in coordinating random assignment and collecting data in a rights-oriented environment.

Community Policing in Houston and Newark. Late in 1982, the
National Institute of Justice (NIJ) (the research arm of the U.S. Department
of Justice) sponsored an evaluation of what has come to be known as
"community policing." Community policing involves organizational and
programmatic adaptations that promise to make law enforcement more
responsive to the needs of communities. This responsiveness is accomplished through organizational changes that open departments to public
input concerning their priorities and procedures, and that adopt a broad,
problem-solving orientation toward local issues.

To find out how well these changes might work, new policing strategies were implemented in neighborhoods in Houston, Texas, and Newark,
New Jersey (for a description of the programs, see Skogan, 1990; Skolnick
and Bayley, 1986). The two cities are extremely different. Houston is a
sprawling, low-density, low-rise, garden-apartment city laid out for easy
access to freeway interchanges. The 380,000 residents of Newark are
packed into nineteen square miles of old wood-frame homes, apartments,
and public housing blocks, arrayed along narrow, crowded streets.

The policing strategies were locally planned, and they reflected differences in the problems targeted for action and in the approaches used to
solve them. The Houston planning task force focused on the lack of contact
police had with ordinary citizens, and on the city's almost nonexistent
neighborhood life. The members of the task force thought that Houston
lacked any sense of local community or tradition of collective self-help,
making it difficult for neighborhoods to respond to disorder and crime.
They also believed that people came into contact with police only under
stressful circumstances that forestalled any informal communication
between them. Newark, on the other hand, ranks near the top on almost
every indicator of big-city problems, and the planning task force decided
that its first objective was to demonstrate that the police still controlled the
streets and could exert their authority to discipline those they considered
out of line. Thus, the list of problems that community policing was to
address turned out to be quite different in each city.

The planning and implementation process also worked quite differently in the two cities, reflecting differences in the organizations and the
local leadership styles. In Newark, the planning and implementation process was "top-down," that is, the command staff of the police department
and outside experts planned their strategies, which were then implemented
by teams of rank-and-file patrol officers under the command of their ser-
geants and district commanders. In Houston, on the other hand, most
elements of the program were designed by a group of patrol officers headed
by a sergeant from the Planning Division of the police department; the
same officers then took charge of individual strategies, recruited a few

more officers from the districts where the program was targeted, and carried out the program themselves. Newark's approach exemplified its traditional, paramilitary management style, while Houston's reflected the police chief's masterplan for departmental decentralization.

These two planning processes produced quite disparate versions of community policing. Houston's program stressed local problem solving and granted the patrol officers in charge a great deal of autonomy. Police opened a storefront office, walked door-to-door gathering information about local problems, fostered local community organizations, wrote and distributed newsletters, and initiated a program serving crime victims. Newark used its preexisting management structure and incorporated more traditional enforcement tactics into its programs. As in Houston, police opened a storefront office and conducted door-step interviews. In addition, they organized harsh crackdowns on street gatherings and public drinking, intensified levels of foot patrol, set up roadblocks to screen drivers for drinking and outstanding warrants, and ejected from buses people who were drinking, eating, or smoking. These activities brought police into direct confrontations with more people than ever before, and the approach was considered very controversial. The crackdowns on street congregations were probably unconstitutional, and the roadblocks were at best heavy-handed (Skolnick and Bayley, 1986).

There were no federal funds to pay for the strategies, so each police chief had to find internal resources, principally personnel, to conduct the programs. In each case it was extremely difficult to justify the disconnecting of officers from the constant stream of incoming emergency or "911" calls. Newark's department shrank by almost 30 percent during the 1970s because the city was virtually bankrupt. To garner enough officers to conduct the program there, it was necessary to reassign administrative personnel to street duty, make staff schedule changes that were in violation of the city's contract with the police union, and push the department's resources to the limit. Newark also tried to involve the school district in a youth recreation component for the program, but in a year the department was unable to overcome bureaucratic obstacles to opening a local school building after dark. Houston's department had not expanded to match the explosive growth of the city during the 1970s, and it was having difficulty answering emergency calls throughout its vast territory. Houston put only a few officers into the pilot projects and ran them virtually without supervision because the chief did not yet have sufficient political and organizational capital to invest more in the effort.

These personnel shortages did make it easy to sell a quasi-experimental design to the police because there was no hope of taking the programs citywide. Areas, not individuals, were allocated to treatment or control status, and as policing is organized along area lines, the fielding of demonstration projects and setting aside of comparison areas fit their mode of thinking.

How did the two planning task forces come up with innovative program plans? The programs in Houston and Newark were formulated with the assistance of the Police Foundation, a research organization based in Washington, D.C., that fosters police innovation. The foundation provided technical assistance to the two departments during their planning effort, which explains some of the similarity of the two programs. Foundation staff "hothoused" the planning process by bringing in outside experts and by having task force members visit successful programs in other cities. Some task force members were trained by professional community organizers and victim services administrators, while others visited cities like Detroit and Santa Ana, California, to talk with officers already involved in community policing. Senior foundation advisers virtually set up residence in each of the cities for almost six months during the planning phase.

The Police Foundation also conducted the evaluation of the programs, taking on a dual role that raised eyebrows in some circles. To facilitate this evaluation, elements of the program were implemented in different areas of Houston and Newark, and one comparison area was identified in each to mark citywide changes. The comparison areas were matched with program areas on several key demographic variables. The evaluation involved observations of the strategies in action, monitoring of events in the cities and in the police departments, interviews with participating officers, and the collection of large amounts of administrative data. (The evaluators, however, were not allowed to read key sections of offense reports made out when people were victimized in the program areas; such openness was judged to be "contrary to departmental policy.")

The success of the projects also needed to be judged along dimensions for which it is difficult to capture routine performance measures. The program was expected to increase police visibility in the target neighborhoods, enhance public confidence in the police, encourage community cohesion and self-help, and reduce fear of crime. Large and expensive sample surveys were conducted in all of the program and comparison areas to measure these outcomes. Since it was not clear at the outset what community policing officers would actually *do* during their year in the field, the surveys included a grab bag of potential process and outcomes measures; at the end of the field period the evaluators then had to negotiate the measures for which each individual team was to be held "responsible" in the report, and which activities should be described but could not be systematically assessed. This process of negotiation greatly increased the program's chances of looking good.

What did the evaluation conclude? Community policing, as implemented in Houston and Newark, showed some success at responding to neighborhood needs. The teams found distinct ways of reaching out for community input and support, and they all succeeded on at least a few of the evaluation measures. The programs in both cities achieved a surprising level of visibility, and in almost every instance disorder went down and citizen satisfaction with their neighborhoods and with the police went up. The traditional enforcement efforts mounted in Newark had few measurable benefits, however, other than driving down levels of visible street disorder.

The worrisome finding of the evaluation was that the benefits of the Houston program largely were confined to whites and home owners of the target areas (see Skogan, 1990). Houston's police chief insisted that selected program neighborhoods have black, Hispanic, and non-Hispanic white residents. This ensured that no ethnic or racial group was "left out" of the program. Analyses of the data from this heterogeneous sample suggested that the program had differential effects. Also for political reasons, the Newark evaluations were conducted only in uniformly poor, black areas, and as a consequence the evaluation had no opportunity to detect treatment interactions by race or class.

Intensive Probation Supervision Programs. The field of corrections is in crisis because of prison overcrowding. The push to alleviate institutional crowding has resulted in the sentencing of serious offenders to a number of "intermediate" treatments short of prison, ranging from harsh "boot camps" (MacKenzie and Shaw, 1990) to fines based on income (Hillsman, 1990) and home confinement (McCarthy, 1987).

One of the most visible intermediate sanctions is intensive probation supervision (IPS). As its name implies, IPS is more strenuous than routine probation. Typically, IPS offenders have multiple weekly contacts with their probation officers; they also are held strictly to curfews and other conditions of release, subjected to unscheduled drug tests, and ordered to perform community service activities (Clear and Hardyman, 1990; Byrne, Lurigio, and Baird, 1989; Lurigio, 1987a). At the beginning of 1990, forty states and Washington, D.C., were administering IPS programs (Byrne, 1990).

The structure of the criminal justice system makes it difficult to conduct MSEs of IPS programs. The greatest difficulties stem from the tremendous diversity of the programs, which is fostered by the decentralization and insularity of that system and by its need to respond to diverse local political concerns (Byrne, Lurigio, and Baird, 1989). IPS programs encompass widely varying goals. Some are "front-end" release mechanisms for prison-sentenced offenders who look eligible for less expensive treatment (Erwin, 1987). Others are "back-end" or early release mechanisms for persons who are already in prison but can be let out at low risk in order to free up prison bed space (Pearson and Harper, 1990). Still others are for felony offenders already sentenced to regular probation who score high on a risk scale that assesses their potential to commit future crimes (Byrne and Kelly, 1989).

IPS programs also employ divergent definitions of "intensive" with respect to supervision (Byrne, Lurigio, and Baird, 1989; Byrne, 1990; Petersilia, 1987). For some programs, intensive only means multiple face-to-face visits with probation officers; for others it means electronically monitored home confinement, curfew checks, periodic imprisonment, visits to employers and family members by investigators, and the payment of restitution to victims. Caseload sizes can range from twelve per officer to forty or more per officer (Tonry and Will, 1988). Programs that appear similar on the surface may emphasize certain elements of casework practices (for example, treatment) over others (for example, surveillance) and may initiate divergent responses to probation violators (offenders who fail to adhere to the conditions of release) (Byrne, 1990; Tonry and Will, 1988).

Another source of differences among IPS programs is their disparate target populations. The programs can involve a broad range of participants, including violent and nonviolent offenders, those at low and at high risk of reoffending, probation and parole violators, and drug offenders (Byrne, 1986). MSEs of IPS programs also are encumbered by a lack of uniform record-keeping practices, a problem that plagues probation and criminal justice agencies in general. In the case of IPS, record keeping often varies with program goals and functions. Back-end early release programs typically involve surveillance and monitor recidivism, whereas front-end programs typically involve treatment and focus on keeping clients out of trouble.

The problem of "net widening" further complicates MSEs of IPS programs. IPS has become such an attractive option to judges that they are sentencing offenders to IPS who would have ordinarily been placed on routine supervision (Lurigio, 1987b). Judges are very sensitive to the adverse repercussions that may ensue from placing prison-bound or high-risk offenders on regular probation (Petersilia and Turner, 1990). For the judiciary, IPS has much more political currency than does traditional probation. The saturation of IPS programs with candidates for regular probation confounds comparisons between intensive and routine probation programs within the same jurisdiction, and it muddles comparisons between IPS programs in different jurisdictions unless evaluators are knowledgeable about the nature and extent of net widening.

IPS programs also serve hidden or latent goals, which are difficult to evaluate. Tonry (1990) identified three unstated functions of IPS. First, it has helped to bolster probation's flagging public relations image by claiming to be tough on offenders. Second, the adoption of IPS has garnered greater resources and esteem for probation officers, who "get to do probation work the way it ought to be done" and "to work closely with just a few people so [they] can make a difference in their lives" (Pearson, 1987, p. 105). Third, IPS strikes a responsive chord with the public's harsher attitudes toward crime and criminals and it does so while attending to fiscal constraints; hence, IPS is infinitely sellable to both politicians and the public.

In short, IPS programs are highly variable with respect to policies and practices. Differences in program goals, operations, personnel, and target populations result in low construct validity (that is, the "intensive" in IPS is defined differently across sites) and in low external validity (that is, the findings from one evaluation may have no relevance or applicability to other programs). Disparities between programs make cross-site comparisons unwieldy and uninterpretable. So far, there has only been one MSE of IPS programs that was able to overcome some of these difficulties. It was not only the first multisite IPS study but also the first to employ randomized experimentation.

In 1986, the Bureau of Justice Assistance (BJA) funded several IPS demonstration projects. To be eligible for funding, sites were required to (1) design their programs in accordance with Georgia's IPS program, which involves reduced caseloads, curfews, employment preparation, drug testing, and community service work; (2) accept only adult offenders; (3) participate in training conferences and technical assistance workshops presented by outside experts; and (4) cooperate in a study designed to evaluate the impact of their programs, which meant collecting a core of data and randomly assigning offenders to the program or routine probation. Eleven sites in seven states were selected for participation. BJA funded evaluations of the programs, which were conducted by the RAND Corporation under the stewardship of Joan Petersilia, director of RAND's Criminal Justice Program (Petersilia and Turner, 1990).

Petersilia (1989) provides a highly informative description of the implementation of the evaluation and useful caveats for future researchers. BJA allocated only $25,000 per site to underwrite the evaluation at each location, which presented serious obstacles to the study; one consequence of the financial constraints was that the programs, independently of each other, had to collect the data and carry out random assignment. RAND researchers were aware that this decision potentially threatened the integrity of the study but concluded that such trade-offs were necessary to undertake the evaluations. In Petersilia's (1989, p. 442) words, "practical realities took precedence over ideal scientific methods."

To bolster their confidence in the soundness of the data and implementation of the research design, RAND staff performed validity checks on the data collected at each site. Petersilia (1989) notes that agency resistance to randomization was overcome primarily by appealing to their self-interest. They were told that random assignment was really the only way to learn about the impact of their efforts and to generate information that they could use persuasively to support the continuation of the program and to establish its credibility. The evaluators also convinced practitioners that random assignment was not capricious but rather an equitable way to make treatment decisions, as there were more eligible offenders than IPS program slots.

To minimize case attrition following random assignment, RAND encouraged the agencies to select offenders late in the process. After reviewing the Federal Judicial Center's (1981) stance on the issue and other legal arguments, the evaluators did not see a compelling obligation to ask clients if they *wanted* to participate in the experiment. This eliminated attrition associated with involuntariness. Finally, RAND only allowed overrides to randomization when judges made special requests to place offenders on IPS; Petersilia (1989) reports that there were only a handful of such cases.

Diffusion of treatment is a serious threat to the internal validity of randomized experiments (Cook and Campbell, 1979). Two strategies were employed to avoid the problem of control group contamination. The first involved explaining to officers the importance of keeping IPS and control interventions as divergent as possible, and the second involved disguising the control cases so that officers would not treat randomly assigned offenders any differently than their other clients. However, a preliminary analysis of program records revealed that treatment and control groups were significantly different on several program-defining variables, such as number of contacts, collateral checks, counseling sessions, and drug tests (Petersilia and Turner, 1990).

RAND researchers could not preclude the emergence of practical differences between the various programs, which undermined their comparability, a major problem in MSEs. Participating agencies were given the latitude to develop IPS along lines compatible with their resources, caseloads, and political contexts. This led to considerable variation across the sites in the operational definition of intensive, procedures, and program clients. For example, only some of the programs had special features such as electronic monitoring and on-site testing. Also, some were designed as prison diversion efforts, whereas others focused on high-risk probationers. At some sites, offenders with any violent convictions or sex offense histories were barred from participation, whereas at others they were included. Because of these differences, Petersilia (1989, p. 440) conceded that "in essence, RAND was conducting 11 different evaluations."

Most of the sites overestimated size of their target populations and had trouble meeting subject quotas during the study period. To compensate for the torpid flow of new clients into IPS, agencies began to downgrade their acceptance criteria so that offenders originally excluded from IPS (for example, drug and violent offenders) later became acceptable. At different sites, there were different shifts in eligibility guidelines, which also commonly resulted in operational changes. For example, when caseloads were light, supervision of those involved was stricter. Researchers at RAND had difficulty keeping pace with the rapidly changing nature of the target populations of the programs. This problem was coupled with uneven screening and referral practices. Program staff were responsible for assessing offenders to determine whether they were eligible for IPS. The evaluators found many instances of failure to refer eligible cases, as well as referrals of cases that were ineligible according to the selection criteria employed.

Despite these obstacles, RAND researchers quickly completed their evaluations of three of the eleven sites. In the California IPS program, random assignment was successful: There were no significant differences between treatment and control groups on demographic measures or indicators of clients' prior records (Petersilia and Turner, 1990). IPS was indeed more intensive than routine probation, as measured by the number and type of contacts and the services provided clients, but IPS offenders had higher rates of technical violations (that is, rule infractions other than new arrests) than did non-IPS offenders. There were no significant differences in rearrest rates between IPS and routine probationers.

Lessons

The community policing and IPS evaluations illustrate a number of the barriers to MSEs erected by the criminal justice system. The decentralization of the system had similar consequences for the community policing and the IPS experiments—although the two sets of programs fell under the same rubric, the actual programs varied widely. Local political, leadership, and resource considerations played as large a role as the program construct in determining what services were actually delivered. IPS was either a substitute for incarceration or a replacement for it, and perhaps it was a punishment for some offenders who otherwise would not have been punished at all. Community policing took on widely divergent targets in different neighborhoods and involved everything from holding meetings in private homes to discussing crime prevention, to cracking down on public drinking by street people.

The fragmented nature of criminal justice policy was reflected in the corrections crisis that brought IPS and other alternatives to incarceration into focus. Legislatures instituted stiffer sentences without funding new prisons; the political push for narcotics enforcement generated millions of new arrests but did not provide judges, jails, or treatment beds. Judges and prosecutors used IPS for varying reasons, producing different client profiles in different jurisdictions. And the lesson of Newark's attempt to coordinate its efforts with that of the school system is a reminder that interagency programs can be very difficult to assemble.

The insular character of the police (in particular) called for expensive technical assistance before they could envision a new way of doing their job. In order to have a program to evaluate, the evaluators had to help organize, educate, and motivate the planning task forces, and to plug them into newly formulated networks of innovative police agencies. The evaluators spent a great deal of time and money ferrying program personnel back and forth between Houston and Newark so that they could reinforce each others' commitment to the program concept and maintain some comparability in projects across the two sites. The evaluators' investment in the resulting programs might have threatened the objectivity with which they were evaluated if the evaluators had not had impartial outsiders monitoring data collection and analyses.

In both cases, the evaluation findings ran afoul of politics. Evidence of success in Houston was sufficiently tainted by suggestions of class and race bias to preclude wide dissemination of results. The community policing MSE could not assess how general this problem of bias might be, however, for political considerations in Newark confined the programs there to poor and homogeneously black neighborhoods. Similarly, RAND released preliminary site-by-site reports of the success of IPS, and there was an uproar because the programs often did not look very successful. Agencies may believe they will be anonymous in an MSE, so in order to avoid this sort of rancor it is important to negotiate in advance the ways in which evaluation data will be analyzed and presented.

New performance measures had to be developed to evaluate the community policing programs, and the data were not the sort that could be collected routinely by any agency. The only data on community policing that were comparable across neighborhoods and cities were gathered in expensive pre- and post-program sample surveys. A change in Houston's computer system meant that even its *own* crime data collected at the time of the MSE were not comparable to those collected in the immediate past. In addition, the iterative and exploratory nature of the program meant that no one was sure what the appropriate measures of process and outcomes would be until well after the pretest survey had been completed. IPS could utilize inexpensive counts of program failures by the agencies involved, but how failure was defined varied from site to site, and in individual cases the definition often hinged on highly discretionary decisions.

Finally, both MSEs faced civil rights issues. In Houston, any interpretation of the evaluation's findings hinges on the weight that is given to the program's differential benefits by race and class. Perhaps as a result, the project's sponsors never widely published the results of the evaluation and gave short shrift to the benefits issue when they did discuss the project. Independent observers doubted not only the constitutionality of some of Newark's efforts but also the propriety of others (Skolnick and Bayley, 1986). Because the program dealt with individual offenders, IPS faced complex legal and professional issues; case workers were to mete out different punishments using decision rules that took into account neither individuals' offenses nor their treatment needs. This practice did not fit any prevailing correctional ideology, and RAND found it difficult to make the case assignment rules stick. To be sure, the criminal justice system itself mostly gives just lip service to its formal norms, which is a source of great frustration to evaluators when those standards are then presented as barriers to their research. In democratic political systems most evaluations examine competing models of care and assess their benefits for the recipients; but in the criminal justice arena it is often the effectiveness of different forms of pain that is under scrutiny, and it is often the apparent benefit of that pain for *other* people, not the subjects of treatment, that determines what shall be done with offenders. Even in their capacity as citizens, evaluators in the criminal justice arena therefore have special responsibilities with regard to how individuals are treated.

References

Byrne, J. M. "The Control Controversy: A Preliminary Examination of Intensive Probation Supervision Programs in the United States." *Federal Probation*, 1986, *50* (3), 4–16.

Byrne, J. M. "Assessing What Works in the Adult Community Corrections System." Paper presented at the annual meeting of the Academy of Criminal Justice Sciences, Denver, Colorado, March 1990.

Byrne, J. M., and Kelly, M. *Restructuring Probation as an Intermediate Sanction: An Evaluation of the Massachusetts Intensive Probation Supervision Program.* Lowell: Center for Criminal Justice Research, University of Massachusetts, 1989.

Byrne, J. M., Lurigio, A. J., and Baird, S. C. "The Effectiveness of the New Intensive Supervision Programs." *Research in Corrections*, 1989, *2* (3), 1–48.

Clear, T. R., and Hardyman, P. L. "The New Intensive Supervision Movement." *Crime and Delinquency*, 1990, *36* (1), 42–61.

Cook, T. D., and Campbell, D. T. *Quasi-Experimentation: Design and Analysis Issues for Field Settings.* Boston: Houghton Mifflin, 1979.

Erwin, B. S. *Evaluation of Intensive Probation Supervision in Georgia.* Atlanta: Georgia Department of Corrections, 1987.

Federal Judicial Center. *Experimentation in the Law: Report of the Federal Judicial Center Advisory Committee on Experimentation in the Law.* Washington, D.C.: Federal Judicial Center, 1981.

Hillsman, S. T. "Fines and Day Fines." In M. Tonry and N. Morris (eds.), *Crime and Justice: A Review of Research.* Chicago: University of Chicago Press, 1990.

Lavrakas, P. J., Rosenbaum, D. P., and Lurigio, A. J. "Media Cooperation with the Police: The Case of Crime Stoppers." In R. Surette (ed.), *The Media and Criminal Justice Policy.* Springfield, Ill.: Thomas, 1990.

Lily, J. R., Ball, R. A., and Wright, J. "Home Incarceration with Electronic Monitoring in Kenton County, Kentucky: An Evaluation." In B. R. McCarthy (ed.), *Intermediate Punishments: Intensive Supervision, Home Confinement, and Electronic Surveillance.* Monsey, N.Y.: Criminal Justice Press, 1987.

Lurigio, A. J. "Evaluating Intensive Probation Supervision." *Perspectives*, 1987a, *11* (1), 17–19.

Lurigio, A. J. "The Perceptions and Attitudes of Judges and Attorneys Toward Intensive Probation Supervision." *Federal Probation*, 1987b, *51* (4), 16–29.

Lurigio, A. J., and Skogan, W. G. "Doing Policy Relevant Research in Criminal Justice Settings: A Tough Road to Hoe." Paper presented at the Illinois Criminal Justice Information Authority's Trends and Issues Conference, Chicago, July 1990.

McCarthy, B. R. (ed.). *Intermediate Punishments: Intensive Supervision, Home Confinement, and Electronic Surveillance.* Monsey, N.Y.: Criminal Justice Press, 1987.

MacKenzie, D. L., and Shaw, J. W. "Inmate Adjustment and Change During Shock Incarceration: The Impact of Correctional Boot Camp Programs." *Justice Quarterly*, 1990, *7* (2), 125–150.

Pearson, F. S. *Research on New Jersey's Intensive Supervision Program.* New Brunswick, N.J.: Dept. of Sociology, Rutgers University, 1987.

Pearson, F. S., and Harper, A. G. "Contingent Intermediate Sentences: New Jersey's Intensive Supervision Program." *Crime and Delinquency*, 1990, *36* (1), 75–86.

Petersilia, J. M. *Expanding Options for Criminal Sentencing.* Santa Monica, Calif.: RAND Corporation, 1987.

Petersilia, J. M. "Implementing Randomized Experiments: Lesson from BJA's Intensive Supervision Project." *Evaluation Review,* 1989, *13* (3), 435–458.

Petersilia, J. M., and Turner, S. "Comparing Intensive and Regular Supervision for High-Risk Probationers: Early Results from an Experiment in California." *Crime and Delinquency,* 1990, *36* (1), 87–111.

Skogan, W. G. *Disorder and Decline: Crime and the Spiral of Decay in American Cities.* New York: Free Press, 1990.

Skolnick, J., and Bayley, D. *The New Blue Line.* New York: Free Press, 1986.

Tonry, M. "Stated and Latent Features of IPS." *Crime and Delinquency,* 1990, *36* (1), 174–191.

Tonry, M., and Will, R. *Intermediate Sanctions.* Castine, Maine: Castine Research Corporation, 1988.

Wesley G. Skogan is professor of political science and a member of the research faculty at the Center for Urban Affairs and Policy Research at Northwestern University, Evanston, Illinois.

Arthur J. Lurigio is a social psychologist. He is currently assistant professor of criminal justice at Loyola University Chicago and research associate at the Center for Urban Affairs and Policy Research, Northwestern University.

The health care arena has a number of unique features that generally facilitate and influence the conduct of multisite evaluations.

Multisite Evaluations of Health Care Policies and Programs

Jay A. Freedman

Health care expenditures in the United States from all sources in fiscal year 1987 represented $500.3 billion or 11.1 percent of the Gross National Product (GNP). Government (federal, state, and local) outlays for health care accounted for almost 40 percent of this total, while private health insurance represented another 31 percent. With so many dollars at stake, it is not surprising that significant research dollars are spent each year to evaluate the cost, quality, efficiency, and efficacy of health care programs and interventions. It is estimated that the United States spends $8.8 billion annually on research in the health care sector. While much of this total is spent on basic research, a growing amount is spent on applied research questions.

While these tremendous expenditures for health care, both in absolute terms and as a percentage of GNP, are a major catalyst for the evaluation of health services programs, the push for large-scale multisite evaluations (MSEs) in this area can be traced to six additional factors: (1) availability of large, multisite data bases, (2) history of multisite clinical trials in biomedical research, (3) highly specialized and educated group of professionals within the health care sector, as well as the dominance of the medical profession, (4) growing evidence that medical care treatment varies across health care settings and regions of the country, (5) growing demand for uniform standards in health care, and (6) growing number of multi-institutional health care systems. In this chapter, these factors are discussed and examples of MSEs of health care policies and programs are described.

NEW DIRECTIONS FOR PROGRAM EVALUATION, no. 50, Summer 1991 © Jossey-Bass Inc., Publishers

Availability of Large, Multisite Data Bases

One factor that facilitates multisite health care evaluations is the availability of large, national data bases. Claims data for medicare, medicaid, and large insurance carriers have made it possible for researchers to investigate variations in health services and resource utilization across various regions of the country, health care providers, and demographic groups. Various public health reporting mechanisms, such as hospital-specific mortality statistics, provide another source of data.

Shift in Focus. A major difficulty in the conduct of MSEs is the task of gaining the cooperation of often-diverse programs that are frequently geographically dispersed and under a variety of organizational auspices. The availability of large, multisite data sets can minimize the time required to gain this cooperation and to coordinate the data collection effort. The availability of these data sets often shifts the focus of MSEs from the development of complex data collection protocols to the development of mechanisms to retrieve existing data, standardize responses across institutions, test for data reliability, and correct for data error.

Wealth of Data. Unlike many other areas of interest to evaluators, the health care sector is awash in data, much of it computerized. Vital statistics, including births, morbidity, and mortality, are routinely collected by the states and the federal government. Hospital discharge abstracts and claims data are required by insurance companies and the government in order for health care providers to receive reimbursement for their services. Other data are collected to comply with legal and certification requirements from groups that accredit health care programs, such as the Joint Commission for Accreditation of Health Care Organizations (JCAHO) and various state agencies. Other health care data that comprise the medical record (either paper or computerized) are generated to facilitate communication, often on a twenty-four-hour basis, between different health care providers: Physicians must be able to pass on instructions to nurses, laboratory technicians, pharmacists, dieticians, and social workers concerning the care and treatment of patients, and day nurses must be able to communicate with night nurses.

In many traditional program evaluations, much time is spent developing and validating measurement instruments, and substantial resources are employed in the collection of data. The availability of large data sets in the health care sector enables evaluators to devote much of their time to the tasks of merging existing data sets, recoding and translating dissimilar coding schemes across medical facilities, and determining data reliability, validity, and bias.

National Data Organizations. This proliferation of health care data has resulted in the creation of organizations such as the National Association of Health Data Organizations, whose purpose is to support the development and use of health care data and to facilitate access to these data. In addition, these organizations promote uniform data standards in the collection, storage, and transmission of health care data. The availability of uniform data standards is another feature of the health care arena that facilitates MSEs.

Designated Data-Processing Staff. One consequence of this data generation activity is that most health care organizations employ a myriad of staff whose primary purpose is the generation, coding, storage, retrieval, and validation of data: ward clerks, fileroom clerks, billing clerks, medical record coders, data entry clerks, computer programmers, medical record reviewers, and data analysts. These employees are critical to the success of MSEs since measurement is central to any evaluation study. Essentially, evaluators collect data that provide the means to measure program process, program outcomes, and program costs. In many program evaluations persons are employed to collect data for evaluation, or existing people are enlisted for this task even though data collection is not their primary responsibility. In many health care evaluations, the evaluator has access not only to data but also to a group of employees whose jobs are to collect, code, store, and validate data.

Data Reliability. The availability of large data sets, however, does not ensure that information contained in such files is either reliable or valid. A study by the Institute of Medicine (1977) to determine the reliability of hospital discharge abstracts compiled by private abstracting services demonstrates this point. These data are generated to provide hospital managers with information on how resources are being used in their medical centers, and to provide information on patient care patterns and resource use for comparable hospitals. Data are abstracted from medical records by hospital personnel when patients are discharged and are then forwarded to the abstracting service for editing and processing. The Institute of Medicine study compared the accuracy of seven information items from each original abstract with an independent review of the original medical record. While the analysis showed that information such as admission date and patient's age and sex were highly reliable, codes for "principal diagnoses combined" agreed only 65.2 percent of the time, and for all procedures the agreement was 73.2 percent (1977, p. 47). Equally troubling, the researchers found that the level of agreement varied significantly across diagnoses, ranging from less than 43.7 percent for a diagnosis of low back pain to 100 percent for personality disorders.

Multisite Clinical Trials

Another facilitating factor for the conduct of MSEs in health care settings is the precedence of multisite clinical trials. While the goal of most MSEs is to ensure adequate population or program diversity, the primary goal of most multisite clinical trails is to ensure a sufficient number of study subjects (Friedman, Furberg, and DeMets, 1982, p. 212). Particularly where the primary variable under investigation is an event that occurs relatively infrequently or where small differences between groups are the focus of the investigation, statistical power may require a very large sample. Multisite clinical trials, while significantly different from MSEs in terms of goals and methods, set the framework for the conduct of MSEs, particularly for those that take place in university-affiliated hospitals.

In a typical multisite clinical trial, the principal investigator, usually a physician working with a coordinating center, identifies and recruits a number of clinical settings for inclusion in the study. These settings are generally headed by research-oriented clinical investigators. Local investigators may participate fully in the development and planning of the multisite clinical trial, or they may have minimal involvement in these activities. In exchange for ensuring patient recruitment into the study and assistance in shepherding the proposal through local human studies and administrative review, the local investigator generally receives investigator status on the protocol as well as co-authorship on subsequent publications. As indicated elsewhere in this volume, local cooperation is essential to the successful conduct of MSEs. Through its participation in multisite clinical trials, a facility can become accustomed to multisite research procedures and practices. To the extent that an MSE complies with these norms, the probability of successful implementation of an MSE at that site will be enhanced.

Because of the tremendous size and cost of multisite clinical trials, organizational structures and procedures have evolved to support the planning and conduct of these studies. For example, the Department of Veterans Affairs Cooperative Studies Program supports four coordinating centers, each employing approximately thirty people, that provide design, data management, statistical analysis, and general administrative support for multisite clinical trials funded by the department. Multisite trials funded by the National Institutes of Health generally provide support for a designated coordinating center. Recently, the Department of Veterans Affairs Health Services Research Program set up two coordinating centers, modeled after their cooperative studies centers, to facilitate multisite health services research.

Highly Educated Employees and the Dominance of the Medical Profession

The highly specialized group of professionals within most health care settings is another feature that distinguishes health care from other service areas of interest to program evaluators. Health care is composed of a vast array of specialized technologies. Each technology requires highly trained professionals to operate and service equipment.

While MSEs may involve a number of different institutional settings, such as hospitals, nursing homes, outpatient clinics, as well as noninstitutional settings, such as visiting nurses or residential care, many of these studies evaluate practice in settings with a high level of physician control. Many authors have noted the professional dominance of the medical profession in health care settings (for example, Freidson, 1970; and Starr, 1982). One of the features that defines physician practice, particularly in academic health care settings, is the overlapping responsibilities of teaching students and conducting research and clinical practice. Thus, the program evaluator conducting an evaluation in a health care setting is surrounded by a variety of professionals, many with solid research expertise. This knowledge can be both a help and a hindrance to the evaluator. On the one hand, the clinical staff members are likely to be sensitive to general issues of measurement and to the rationale for randomization and control groups. On the other hand, the clinical staff, particularly if they define research in terms of clinical trials and bench research, may be less tolerant of the "softer" methods often employed by evaluators, such as surveys, focus groups, and psychometric scales.

Evidence That Medical Care Treatment Varies Across Health Care Settings and Regions of the Country

As previously indicated, one goal of MSEs is to control for programmatic, patient, social, and economic differences that can influence the outcomes of health care interventions. If personal and professional health care practices did not vary across sites or areas of the country, the need for MSEs would be limited to those occasions where the condition under study is so rare that multiple centers are required to ensure an adequate sample size. However, a number of studies have shown that medical practices, health care utilization, and health care costs vary significantly across institutions and regions of the country.

Wennberg and Gittelsohn (1982) examined the rate of surgery in 193 small areas in the six states of New England. The investigators, using computerized hospital discharge abstracts, found that the rates of surgery for the three most common surgical procedures (hysterectomy, prostatectomy, and tonsillectomy) varied by as much as a factor of six between the highest and lowest rate areas (1982, p. 120).

Mitchell and Davidson (1989), using claims data from ten states, examined surgical fees for six operations, representing three types of surgery (cardiovascular, orthopedic, and general). Each procedure was assigned to a metropolitan statistical area (MSA) or a non-MSA based on the location of the physician's practice. Differences between the highest and lowest charge areas ranged from 59 percent for a hip replacement to 244 percent for a pacemaker insertion. When these fees were adjusted for geographically based cost differences (for example, physician and employee time, rent, and malpractice insurance), the differences between high-charge and low-charge areas were reduced to 46 percent for coronary artery bypass graft and 214 percent for pacemaker insertion. The investigators also found that there were no consistent patterns across surgical procedures, that is, areas with high fees for one surgical procedure had low fees for other surgeries.

Growing Demand for Uniform Standards in Health Care

As indicated above, utilization rates, practice patterns, and health care costs vary significantly across health care settings and areas of the country, resulting in increased interest in MSEs in the health care area. Such evidence has also increased the demands from the government, purchasers of health services, and the public at-large for uniform standards of care. These uniform standards require uniform, data collection protocols, which provide additional incentives for MSEs. Groups that accredit health care facilities, such as JCAHO, are moving from a process of peer review to criteria-based audits and, ultimately, to large-scale performance-based statistical comparisons of health care organizations (JCAHO, 1988).

Growing Number of Multi-Institutional Health Care Systems

The growth in multi-institutional health care systems in the 1980s is another source of support for MSEs. For example, in 1987 46 percent of all community hospitals were part of multihospital systems, up from 31 percent in 1979. Nursing homes have seen a similar growth in multi-institutional systems. In 1985, 41 percent of all nursing home facilities were affiliated with chains (representing almost 50 percent of all nursing home beds), an increase from 38 percent in 1977 (Strahan, 1987). In addition, changes in reimbursement have resulted in the development of new organizational structures, such as preferred provider organizations, that provide access to shared data across health care providers.

Multi-institutional health care systems encourage MSEs, in part because these systems are more likely to be able to afford the staffs and attract the program evaluators, health services researchers, computer programmers, and biostatisticians necessary to conduct high-quality evaluative studies. The Department of Veterans Affairs Health Services Research and Development Service and the Hospital Corporation of America's Center for Health Studies are examples of this phenomenon of support for MSEs. In addition, management of these multi-institutional systems encourages the development of common data elements, common file structures, and common data communication protocols to measure performance across facilities. As we have seen, the availability of large, multisite data sets often encourages multisite studies.

Finally, the sheer size of many of these health care systems can make the evaluation of even minor changes in practice cost-effective and, therefore, worthy of study.

Types of Multisite Evaluations

Broadly speaking, MSEs can be grouped into four categories. These categories can be thought of as "ideal types." While most health services MSEs will have aspects of more than one of these study categories or types, they will tend to more closely approximate one category over the others.

Studies That Depend Solely on Secondary Data Sources for Evaluation of Policies and Programs. Many of these studies are conducted with the investigator never setting foot in a health care facility and never collecting even a fragment of original data. Because detailed site-specific data are rarely available from secondary data sources, this kind of evaluation is more generally applied to broad-based economic and social policies rather than to specific programmatic initiatives.

The work of Wennberg and Gittelsohn (1982) is typical of this type of MSE. The investigators utilized computerized records of hospital admissions for the states of Maine, Rhode Island, and Vermont, which included such information as the patient's age, sex, place of residence, diagnoses, surgical procedures, and dates of admission and discharge. Data from independent studies for the states of Connecticut, Massachusetts, and New Hampshire were used, supplemented by Medicare data. By looking at each patient's residence location (by ZIP code), as well as the location where hospital treatment was provided, hospital treatment areas were defined.

From these data, 193 hospital areas were defined with populations of between 10,000 and 200,000. By counting the surgical procedures done on the population within a hospital area in a given time period, the per capita rate for a surgical or medical procedure can be calculated. Insurance reimbursement rates can also be calculated in this way.

As noted earlier, the availability of large, national data sets does not ensure that the information contained in such files is either valid or reliable. In addition, the sheer size of these data sets can create problems. If the number of cases in a data set is large enough, even very weak relationships will be statistically significant. In addition, if data sets contain a large number of variables, there may be a tendency for investigators to "fish" for statistically significant relationships. If the significance is set at the $p < .05$ level, 5 percent of the relationships examined can be statistically significant by chance alone. Finally, in both the Wennberg and Gittelsohn (1982) and the Mitchell and Davidson (1989) studies, the unit of analysis is a geographical area, and the data collected concern individual patient encounters with a physician. Many of their analyses depended on the calculation of a rate that is the number of procedures or encounters divided by the population within an area. These calculations were based on the assumptions that an individual can only have a procedure once per a given time period and that the entire population for an area is the appropriate denominator for calculating the rate.

Studies That Depend on the Labor of Existing Program Staff for Data Collection. Obviously, to get overburdened program staff to collect study data requires the support of organization managers. Generally, these MSEs are the products of in-house evaluation units whose knowledge of the organizations' standard operating procedures and familiarity with management personnel help secure the compliance of lower-level staff in the data collection effort. As previously described, medical organizations collect a myriad of information. The validity and reliability of these data are often questioned and, to some extent, are driven by the purposes for which they were originally collected. While data collected by an organization may be valid for and meet the needs of that organization, the same data may not be valid for the purposes of the program evaluator.

In the early 1980s there was growing concern about the ability of the Veterans Administration (VA) (now the Department of Veterans Affairs) to meet the health care needs of its client population. Existing data indicated that no veteran who required medical care and who was entitled to care was being denied health services. Yet, stories persisted, suggesting that some veterans were being turned away from necessary care. As a result, a study was commissioned in 1984 (Demakis and others, 1990) to determine the degree to which the VA was meeting the health care needs of veterans who sought care at VA facilities. The study, eventually conducted by the VA Health Services Research and Development Field Program at Hines VA Hospital, located outside of Chicago, focused on four areas of health care demand: (1) applications for care through the admissions office (regardless of the type of care required—inpatient, outpatient, or nursing home—veterans requesting treatment apply for care through the admissions offices of VA hospitals or freestanding clinics), (2) telephone requests for transfer from non-VA health care sources to the VA for patient or outpatient care, (3) waiting times for clinic appointments in selected VA clinics, and (4) early discharges from outpatient clinics for patients still requiring care.

While data were collected by the VA on an ongoing basis for the number of applications for care and clinic discharges, information on the medical needs of these patients was either not collected or else was collected, but on an administrative basis and not on clinical grounds. Under the accounting system in effect at that time, veterans who were not eligible to receive care under VA regulations but who required ongoing care, for example, patients with chronic stable conditions, might be classified as not requiring care.

As in many studies conducted by in-house evaluators, data collection was the responsibility of existing administrative staff. Letters were sent to the directors of all VA medical centers describing the purpose of the survey and instructing each of them to appoint both an administrative and a physician coordinator for the survey. To facilitate control of data quality, the names, positions, and telephone numbers of selected staff were then sent to the survey coordinating center. One reason for requesting both an administrative and clinical coordinator for the survey was to more accurately determine the clinical needs of patients who were seeking care but were denied care. It was also hoped that the involvement of two individuals in the completion of each survey form would further encourage the respondents to be accurate. Finally, the survey indicated in several places that a randomly selected group of hospitals would be resurveyed by outside auditors to determine survey accuracy.

As an in-house study, the various surveys had a response rate of 100 percent. Audits conducted by the survey staff and computerized checks for data consistency found a number of data errors or inconsistencies. Using the names and phone numbers recorded on the returned surveys, most of these errors were corrected prior to data analysis.

Auditors went to twenty-four randomly selected VA medical centers and independently examined the charts of patients who were not admitted to the hospital or who were not given return appointments. The auditors were blind to the original survey reports. With respect to applications through the admissions offices, there was an overall agreement rate of 78 percent between the auditors and the original survey reports. In the case of veterans who were discharged from VA clinics, there was an overall agreement rate of 91 percent. Audits were not possible for the telephone requests for transfer or the surveys of clinic waiting times.

Studies That Combine Secondary Data Sources with Original Data Collection. As previously noted, original data collection at multiple sites is a costly and time-consuming endeavor, whereas secondary analysis of existing data may severely limit the range of evaluation questions addressed and the level of analysis performed. The strategy of combining aspects from both of these approaches, that is, combining secondary analysis of existing data with original data collection, can provide a mechanism to sharpen the focus of analysis, while minimizing the overall cost of the evaluation. The evaluation of the Medicaid program (Davidson, Perloff, Kletke, Schiff, and Connelly, 1982; Perloff, Kletke, and Neckerman, 1987) is an example of this type of MSE.

A major goal of the Medicaid program, which was created in 1965, was to ensure access for poor people to high-quality health care. This access was promoted through the availability of funds to purchase needed health services. Patients who qualify for care under the program need only identify physicians willing to treat them, and the Medicaid program pays for the care provided. However, the availability of funds alone does not ensure access to needed care. In order for the system to work, physicians must be willing to participate in the state-run programs and provide care under the constraints and conditions imposed by the system. Since states retain broad discretionary power over Medicaid policy and vary with respect to eligibility criteria, covered services, and levels of reimbursement, a multistate analysis of Medicaid programs provides a natural experiment to evaluate the impact of various program policies on physician participation.

In 1978 (Davidson, Perloff, Kletke, Schiff, and Connelly, 1982) and again in 1983 (Perloff, Kletke, and Neckerman, 1987), approximately eight hundred office-based pediatricians were surveyed about their Medicaid participation and other aspects of their medical practices. Pediatricians were selected using a stratified random sample in thirteen states. States were carefully selected to yield a diverse range of Medicaid characteristics.

The 1978 survey utilized telephone interviews to elicit information about the pediatricians sampled, their practices, their attitudes and opinions, and their experiences with the Medicaid program. The 1983 follow-up study utilized mailed questionnaires adapted from the 1978 interviews. To construct state Medicaid case studies, a variety of secondary data sources were employed, including socioeconomic characteristics by state and ZIP code areas from the Bureau of the Census, county and state health resources, and socioeconomic information from the Bureau of Health Manpower. Characteristics of state Medicaid programs, such as eligibility criteria, covered services, and methods of reimbursement, came from a number of sources, including the Social Security Administration, the Health Care Financing Administration, and the Bureau of Labor Statistics.

Studies That Primarily Depend on Original, Evaluation-Specific Data Collection. While this is the preferred mode for evaluating health interventions, the costs and logistical difficulties associated with undertaking this type of MSE restrict the number of studies actually undertaken. The evaluation of adult day health care discussed by Hedrick and her colleagues (this volume) is an example of this type of MSE. One factor that facilitated the conduct of this MSE was that all of the sites studied were part of a national system of health care, the Department of Veterans Affairs, which eased coordination of and access to patients and data. The growth of multi-institutional health care settings noted elsewhere in this chapter may further facilitate MSEs. While much of the data for the evaluation of adult day health care were collected by researchers hired by the study team, the sources for much of these data were existing hard copy and computerized files.

Conclusion

Evaluators in the health care arena have a number of assets at their disposal that can facilitate the development and management of MSEs. Availability of national data sets, highly trained staffs of data collectors and encoders, precedents of multisite clinical trials, growth in multi-institutional health care systems, and growing demands for uniform standards of care are all factors that can facilitate the conduct of MSEs. However, these same factors, if misused, can undermine the evaluation effort. Existing national data sets composed of unreliable data or data that do not adequately represent the construct under study can seriously harm an MSE. Employees that are enlisted to collect data for which they do not see the merit or for whom adequate inducements have not been developed can also undermine the study protocol. Systematic monitoring of data quality is crucial to any evaluation, but it is essential in an MSE.

References

Davidson, S., Perloff, J., Kletke, P., Schiff, D., and Connelly, J. "Variations by State in Physician Participation in Medicaid." Final Report Grant No. 18-P-97159/5. Baltimore, Md.: Health Care Financing Administration, 1982.

Demakis, J., Turpin, R., Conrad, K., Stiers, W., Weaver, F., Sinacore, J., Cowper, D., Darcy, L., Huck, M., Friedman, B., Freedman, J., and Sherman, S. "The Whole Is Greater Than the Sum of Its Parts: The Anatomy of the Department of Veterans Affairs Medical District 17 Health Services Research and Development Field Program." *Health Services Research*, 1990, *25* (1), 269–285.

Freidson, E. *Professional Dominance.* New York: Atherton, 1970.

Friedman, L., Furberg, C., and DeMets, D. *Fundamentals of Clinical Trials.* Boston: John Wright, 1982.

Institute of Medicine. *Reliability of Hospital Discharge Abstracts.* Washington, D.C.: National Academy of Sciences, 1977.

Joint Commission on Accreditation of Healthcare Organizations (JCAHO). *Guide to Quality Assurance.* Chicago: JCAHO, 1988.

Mitchell, J., and Davidson, S. "Data Watch: Geographic Variation in Medicare Surgical Fees." *Health Affairs*, 1989, *8* (4), 113–124.

Perloff, J., Kletke, P., and Neckerman, K. *Medicaid and Pediatric Primary Care.* Baltimore, Md.: Johns Hopkins University Press, 1987.

Starr, P. *The Social Transformation of American Medicine.* New York: Basic Books, 1982.

Strahan, G. "Nursing Home Characteristics: Preliminary Data from the 1985 National Nursing Home Survey." *NCHS Advance Data from Vital and Health Statistics.* Department of Health and Human Services Publication No. (PHS) 87-1250. Hyattsville, Md.: National Center for Health Statistics, 1987.

Wennberg, J., and Gittelsohn, A. "Variations in Medical Care Among Small Areas." *Scientific American*, 1982, *246* (4), 120–134.

Jay A. Freedman is coordinator of Health Services Research and Development at the Veterans Affairs Medical Center, Indianapolis, Indiana, and assistant professor in the Department of Medicine, Indiana University, Indianapolis.

INDEX

ORDERING INFORMATION

NEW DIRECTIONS FOR PROGRAM EVALUATION is a series of paperback books that presents the latest techniques and procedures for conducting useful evaluation studies of all types of programs. Books in the series are published quarterly in Fall, Winter, Spring, and Summer and are available for purchase by subscription as well as by single copy.

SUBSCRIPTIONS for 1991 cost $48.00 for individuals (a savings of 20 percent over single-copy prices) and $70.00 for institutions, agencies, and libraries. Please do not send institutional checks for personal subscriptions. Standing orders are accepted.

SINGLE COPIES cost $15.95 when payment accompanies order. (California, New Jersey, New York, and Washington, D.C., residents please include appropriate sales tax.) Billed orders will be charged postage and handling.

DISCOUNTS FOR QUANTITY ORDERS are available. Please write to the address below for information.

ALL ORDERS must include either the name of an individual or an official purchase order number. Please submit your order as follows:
   Subscriptions: specify series and year subscription is to begin
   Single copies: include individual title code (such as PE1)

MAIL ALL ORDERS TO:
   Jossey-Bass Inc., Publishers
   350 Sansome Street
   San Francisco, California 94104

FOR SALES OUTSIDE OF THE UNITED STATES CONTACT:
   Maxwell Macmillan International Publishing Group
   866 Third Avenue
   New York, New York 10022

OTHER TITLES AVAILABLE IN THE
NEW DIRECTIONS FOR PROGRAM EVALUATION SERIES
Nick L. Smith, *Editor-in-Chief*